The Other Half

Sue Whitehead

First edition published in 2003 by
New Life Publishing, 15 Barking Close
Luton, Beds. LU4 9HG
orders@goodnewsbooks.net

from articles originally printed in
Goodnews Magazine

British Library Cataloguing in Publication Data
A catalogue record for this book is
available from the British Library

References taken from the
New International Version of the Bible

ISBN 1 903623 10 3

Cover design by Yvonne Bell, 02380 773271. Yvonne creates Stoles,
Chausables and Copes to individual design, often on silk - as for the
cover of this book. She paints Icons, Celtic motifs and Medieval
illuminations, designs Church banners and Christmas cards and
illustrates the Gospel message.   www.vestments.co.uk

Typesetting by New Life Publishing.
Printed in the UK by Cromwell Press Limited,
Trowbridge, Wilts.

to Charles who really is
my better half and to
my Dad who showed me
unconditional love

Contents

Foreword i

Prologue...iii

Pearls of Wisdom...1

A Dictator?... Who... Me?....................................3

Through the Doubts...5

I Only Asked ! 7

Expectant Love..8

What if ..... ? 9

Passover..10

Hand in Hand 12

Constancy...14

Missed Turnings 15

Separation 16

Suffering Miserably 17

The Greatest Sign 18

The Mountain of the Lord....................................20

More Discipline ! 22

Inner Child 24

We Saw His Glory 26

Dare We Step Out in Faith ? 28

Thoughtful Giving 30

Plan Well and Accept Change 31

Turning to the Son-Light 33

Because of Jesus 35

Heart Cleansing 36

Most Precious Child 39

Contents continued ...

Hungry for God's Word 40
Starting the Day Right 41
Passing Time 43
Trials 45
Prioritising My Time 47
All In a Name 49
God's Colours 51
Inner Disabilities 52
Free Choice 54
The Power of God 56
He Loves Us to Pieces 58
Living Colours 60
Called By Name 62
Informed Faith 64
Pearls 65
Blessed by Life 67
Spiritual Top-Up 69
A Free Gift 71
The Christian Family 73
The Heart of Belief 74
Promises 75
Rushing to Judgement 77
The Joy of Belonging 79
A Bridge to God 80
Small Things 81

Contents continued ...

Unclouded Judgement 83
Concentrate your mind.......................................85
The Cross 87
The Family of God 88
Unconditional Love 89
Sunday Christian 90
Speaking Positively 92
Washed By the Spirit 94
Momentous Night 95
Standing My Ground 96
A Year of Favour 97
Material Sacrifices 98
Facing Challenges - With God 100
Love and Forgiveness 102
An Attitude of Gratitude 103
God Among Us 104
A Phone Line to God 105
Joy in the Lord 107
Tradition 109
Listening to the Spirit 110
Wait for the Lord 112
God Has No Favourites 114
Smile - God Loves You ! 116
Made With Love 119
Who Are You? 120
Epilogue 123

Foreword

It's always a privilege to be asked to write a foreword to a book, and when the author is my 'other half' it's a special, if rather unusual, pleasure. When I then consider that our children, other members of our family, friends and acquaintances, and some shared moments in our lives, have all provided material for different chapters, it becomes a much more interesting exercise than writing a normal foreword - not to mention the fact that I happen to know the author rather well!

The Other Half has appeared in the Goodnews magazine for over twelve years, but it's much more than a collection of anecdotes. I know that through each of the incidents recounted, the Lord has spoken to Sue and she has done her best to convey to the reader what she's learned. The stories are usually amusing, sometimes challenging and painful, but always real, and it's this realism and honesty that characterises Sue's writing.

I've been pleasantly surprised on many occasions when Goodnews readers have told me that they so enjoy and appreciate *The Other Half* that it's the first thing they turn to. I well remember attending a conference in Italy a few years ago, and sitting at breakfast with a prominent African Archbishop and a well-known Bishop from northern India. One of them began to recount a story, only to find he was interrupted and corrected from time to time by the other. When he got to the end, the Archbishop asked the Bishop where he had heard the story. As they both realised the answer, they roared with laughter as they turned to me 'Sue told it in the latest issue of Goodnews!' They both admitted they had already used the story in homilies at Sunday Mass, one in

Africa and the other in India, and I was amused to think that *The Other Half* must have reached some unexpected places. But then such stories aren't limited by time, place, or culture, and I'm delighted they've been brought together in a book, and are now certain to travel even further afield.

So I'm sure that wherever you are you'll enjoy reading this little book, and that it will remind you of the many ways the Lord speaks to us in the midst of our busy lives - in the normal everyday things just as much as in the more obviously spiritual activities in which we engage. I know it has not always been easy to write, but it's been done with much love, and with the one desire that it will be a help and a blessing to those who read it, and will thereby bring glory to the one who alone makes sense of all the ups and downs of life - Jesus, the King of Kings and the Lord of Lords.

Charles Whitehead
February 2003

Prologue

I'd just like to tell you a few things before you start reading!

I never planned to write this book, because I never think of myself as a writer. Admittedly when I was younger I had a few good ideas (I thought) for novels, which would become classics and be made into remarkable films bringing me to vast wealth and fame, but I never did actually put pen to paper so obviously that never happened. Then I started writing **The Other Half** for Goodnews. Sometimes there were lots of things to write and I would do two or three together, but usually I found myself near the deadline praying for God to give me an inkling of the next article! It's amazing how God really IS in everything we hear, do and say, and I am continually surprised by the nudges He gives me in everyday life.

It was the same sort of scenario with the doodles. When I was at school I was told I couldn't draw. Actually, I think I suspected that myself, as my 'art' productions were the result of major concentration and little creativity. One day I was at a conference and the speaker said something about the father heart of God and immediately in my mind I saw the picture. I decided to copy it on my pad; it's not brilliant - as you'll see on page 34 - but it was the beginning of believing that I could put on paper the pictures in my head. All the doodles happened while I listened to speakers. I always took my little sketch pad with me but never tried to draw until the picture to be copied came to mind. Underneath the drawings I've written the words that started the picture or sometimes the name of the place where I was.

I wanted to tell you all this as an encouragement to any of you who have been told 'you can't do that'. You never know!

So I gave all the bits to Toni & Gerard, my publishers, and they have put it all together. I really am most grateful to them and I hope you'll enjoy it. I hope that no one will be offended by anything I have written, nor by how I have written it. The Lord has a wonderful sense of humour and learning to laugh helps us so much. And don't worry if you see me looking at you a bit strangely next time we meet. I might just be thinking: 'that's another *Other Half* moment'!

Sue

Sue Whitehead
February 2003

PEARLS OF WISDOM

Just this week I was talking to Mrs Simpson, Tom's teacher.

Apparently, the class had been reading a story about a Genie in a bottle who had granted his rescuer three wishes, and the children had then been asked to write out three wishes which they would like to make if they were ever 'Genie liberators'! Tom had approached Mrs Simpson's desk, task completed, and this is how she related it to me.........

Tom had written for his third wish - to wish to be a millionaire. Just as Mrs Simpson was going to comment, he grabbed the piece of paper and said, 'I'd better add something to that.' She watched, intrigued, as he returned to his desk and scribbled furiously, curious to know what brilliant thought had struck. On his return she read the amended wish - 'I wish to be a millionaire so that I could give some money to the poor.' Impressed, she looked at Tom but before she could say anything, he shrugged his shoulders, lifted his hands and said, 'Well, if I was rich, my mother'd make me anyway!'

As she finished telling me, we both laughed and she said, 'I thought you'd like to know that something is rubbing off on him.'

I was glad to know - so often what we say to the children seems to pass unheard, let alone unheeded! When I think of the pearls of wisdom that have dropped from my lips and rolled ignored before my beloved offspring over the past few years! When I remember the times that they could have avoided hurts and disappointments if only they had listened to my advice! Funny that - I vaguely

1

remember my mother saying similar things to me many years ago. I suppose, in the end, each generation learns anew each time.

So, it is very good to hear that Tom is learning early - maybe it's because lately it hasn't been just words; maybe, just lately, we've begun to live what we say.

...the fruit of the Spirit is love, joy, peace, patience, kindness, goodness, faithfulness, gentleness, and self-control.
Galatians 5:22

A DICTATOR......? WHO.... ME?

Quite recently we had an interesting insight into how the children see us! Luke spent an hour and a quarter in a car with Tommy, a young friend of ours, and by the end Tommy reckoned he knew exactly how to handle Charles and me!

Apparently, Luke had informed him that if he and Tom (that's our Tom) wanted anything, the best bet was to ask Charles first, because he was easier to talk round - a doleful expression and yearning eyes carried a lot of weight, said the expert - but even with him 'on side', it was not always possible to get it past me! If I said 'NO' that was it; a "NO' from Mum was a 'NO'. This was said with all the seriousness of a ten year old's wisdom - a fact to be accepted and lived with!

I protested quite volubly that I wasn't a dictator at all; I was always open to a rational argument.   Apparently that is not so!!!   The consensus of opinion around the family - Charles, Lucy, Adam, and the two instigators of this enquiry - is that it's a pretty accurate description of reality!

So, should I change? That's the big question. Could it be true that every decision I make is not correct? I find that hard to believe!! I take so many factors into consideration before I speak, don't I? Well, here comes the good old escape line - I try my best!

I am trying to listen to all the arguments these days, without having made up my mind already. Of course, the little ones don't know it yet but I'm not really immovable - Charles and I do have discussions without them (afterwards) and I have often agreed with him eventually! It's good that we are a family of Love and even in the 'NO-ing' the 'Loving' is predominant.

It's working well just now but I think I'll wait a while before I admit I'm not infallible - after all, Lucy and Adam found out soon enough.

THROUGH THE DOUBTS

A few years ago we had a very 'holy' year. Luke was then 8 years old and preparing to receive his first communion. He was beginning to open his life to Jesus but, on the way, he managed to ask some quite difficult questions. One such arose when he, Tom, and I were returning from the airport. It was the week before the big day so I suppose it was natural that Luke should have been thinking about it. Anyway the questions started.....

'Will Lucy and Adam come to church with us on Saturday?' (our older two rarely joined us other than at Easter and Christmas).
'Oh yes, they'll be there.'
'Will they receive communion?'
'No, I don't think so.'
"Haven't they made their first communion yet?'
'Yes, when they were your age, but they don't go now.'
'Why not?'

(Charles, I thought, how can you be on a plane leaving me to cope with this!) I took a deep breath:

'Well, when they were young they knew Jesus and knew that He was their friend and, like you, they tried to do what He wanted; but as they got older they found they didn't always want to do what He'd want so they stopped talking to Him in case he said something they didn't want to hear. They decided to be in charge of their own lives, which meant they ignored Jesus.'
'That must make Jesus very sad.'
'I think it does.'
'We must pray for them.'
'That's right, we must.'

There was a brief pause:

'I've had my doubts about Jesus, you know, - but I'm through that now.'

'I've never had any doubts,' piped up Tom, the previously silent five year old!

Dear God, may these two always be shining lights for you. May they never turn away to walk their own paths. Help them to cope with the peer pressure they'll encounter and may the reality of their faith be such that it will never be shaken. Help us to share your love with Lucy and Adam so that they, too, will come 'through the doubts'.

I ONLY ASKED!

I'd collected the boys from school and was driving home. We were discussing the day and Luke said .....

'David and I were talking about Jesus today - I said that he'd died on the cross to heal people. Was that right?'

'Mmmmm, sort of.' I said. 'While Jesus walked around on the earth He healed the people He met and now He wants us to pray for those who are ill, to bring them to Him to be healed. And he died on the cross so that we could be friends again with God, our Father. You see, when God created men they were really good friends but after a while, men decided to do what they wanted and not what God wanted so they turned away and did their own thing, and then God was very sad. He couldn't be friends with them any more, because God, being only good, cannot be with anything bad. So Jesus said - 'Let me do something about it. Let me put it right.' And when He was dying on the cross He said - 'Blame me for everything that they've done wrong. All the wrong things that Luke's done, that Sue's done, that Tom's done. Blame me and then you can be friends with them again.' Do you understand that?'

I looked in the driving mirror and saw my son's face with eyes wide open and eyebrows raised.

'I only asked a question,' he said. 'Yes or No would have done.'

EXPECTANT LOVE

Recently, I went to a conference without Charles. I'd not done that before and although it was great to be there, and I was with friends, I felt somewhat incomplete. On the third day I spoke to Charles and he agreed to come up for the evening session, and what a difference that made. I 'praised' better and I concentrated hard, knowing that I would be seeing him soon! As the time for his arrival drew near I could hardly keep still. When I saw him coming into the crowded hall, my heart truly gave a 'fillip' of joy! Being 'in love' has an interesting effect, to say the least.

I remember the first 'falling in love'. I was only about ten years old and he was 15 years. I saw him across the church at Sunday School. I found out what colours he liked - and chose my dresses accordingly. I thought about him an awful lot, and he didn't even notice my existence.

How different it is to be in love with Jesus who knows me and loves me. I know He never leaves me and yet, sometimes, I feel I'm waiting, looking for Him over and over and over and over again - I don't ever want to lose that first expectant longing, to be what He wants and to be where He is.

WHAT IF........?

It was Charles' turn the other day to cope with one of Luke's logical thinking bouts! Luke appeared from the garden -

'Dad, what would have happened if Adam hadn't eaten the apple? I mean, there wouldn't have been any sin and they wouldn't have been thrown out of the garden, so the garden would have been heaven, wouldn't it? And there wouldn't have been any death, so it would have been overcrowded - right? And Jesus wouldn't have had the job to do so He'd have been very bored, wouldn't He?'

For Luke, to be bored is the worst he can imagine!

Charles was sure that, somewhere in there, the logic wasn't quite right! We've talked about it a lot: it's quite a good conversational gambit! It's nice to think that man might never have fallen but we suspect that, sooner or later, Adam would have chosen his own way and not the Lord's. One thing I'm sure of - Jesus is neither bored nor boring. We keep telling the boys that only boring people get bored, and from all we know of the Lord, that adjective just doesn't fit. And I think it will be very nice in heaven if it IS crowded - crowded with those I know and love, and with lots of folks who've gone before, all related in Christ. So many people to meet - I wonder what Adam is like?

PASSOVER

This year, a lovely lady in our parish decided to organise a Passover meal for the children. When we arrived at the church hall I must confess that I listened to the noise of 100 children finding seats, shouting to their friends, and I wondered what on earth it would be like! The twelve chosen 'disciples' took their places at the top table, on the stage, and when our parish priest, who was Jesus for the day, walked in, an expectant silence fell. He talked a little about the setting and the tradition, which the Jewish families still follow; he lit the candles and asked the 'disciples' to prepare the table.

As they brought the lamb-bone, bitter herbs, salt water, green veg.(lettuce), matzo and charoset (a sweet paste), they held them up for everyone to see. When the table was laid, the youngest 'disciple' began to ask the ritual questions and we started to experience the Jewish memories. We recalled the bitterness of their slavery and the tears they shed; we remembered the bricks they had to make and the pain they suffered. The matzo reminded us how there had been no time to wait for the bread to rise on that first 'Passover' and we remembered the lamb that was killed, it's blood put over the doorway as a sign.

And I haven't seen 100 children so engrossed and interested for a long time - they tasted the horseradish and it made their eyes smart; the lettuce dipped in salt water! They ate the sweet paste (apple!) and were surprised to find that they quite liked the matzo. They really listened to the questions and answers and will, I'm sure, grow up with a small understanding of the Jewishness of Our Lord. Maundy Thursday really was special this year and it was a privilege to share it with the children. After the ritual they enjoyed a feast of chicken, pizza and cakes (slightly updated fare!). I was standing near the top table when a helper asked the 'disciples' if they knew which 'disciple' they were meant to be:

'Oh yes - I'm Thomas,' said Tom
'And I'm St. Peter,' said his friend, Peter.
'O.K' said the six year old next to them, 'I'll be St. Habib.'

I think Jesus would have liked that!

Set my heart on fire
Jan 10 '95

HAND IN HAND

Recently I had to give a talk around a Bible verse which was about holding God's hand and I found myself watching people shopping with children. It was fascinating to see the different relationships and I think that there were three basic ways that they walked together. You'll probably recognise the descriptions!

1. Parents holding child's hand, walking together. They talked to each other, laughed - obviously enjoying each other's company. They discussed the choices before them and appeared to make decisions together, although I could recognise that the parent had the over-riding vote, exercised in love and understood by both. There was a harmony about them and it really was a pleasure to see their mutual happiness.

2. Child holding parent's hand but desperately trying to get away. Darting forwards and backwards to look here and there and everywhere. Picking things up, putting things down, causing chaos - more or less 'doing their own thing.'

3. Definitely a very reluctant shopper! The parent struggled to move on while the child hung back, really impeding the forward motion - sometimes even managing to hook an arm around an upright to stop the progress completely.

You'll understand that most children fell into the last two categories!

And I began to draw the parallel with how we walk with our Father God.

So often when we walk with Him we're trying desperately to do things 'our way' - we have our own ideas of 'how to do it'. Or maybe we really don't want to move on from where we are and we hold on to happenings or experiences from the past because we 'know them' and feel safe.

In these parent/child pictures I realised that there are faults on both sides - the parent, too, contributes to the problem. But with our perfect Father, all the problems are of our own making.

Perhaps, occasionally, we walk with our Father holding His hand, trusting Him and believing He knows the best way to do things. We communicate with Him and wait for His guidance - and when we do, we experience the joy, peace, and happiness of a fulfilled relationship.

And I bet other people notice!

Take my heart,
O Lord

CONSTANCY

This Lent, Luke decided to give up Hobnobs. That might not sound a great hardship to some of us but, every day after school, the treat is two plain chocolate Hobnobs to stave off hunger pangs before tea. Over the years we've tried to encourage a positive attitude to Lent, for example: 'I shall try to give up provoking my brother into an argument' ..... so this was a new approach.

Anyway, this year, Luke announced his decision. This was doubly hard as Tom said he did not think *he* would give them up so would I please still provide them for him! As you can imagine this made it quite difficult for Luke each day as, not only did he not eat them, but he also had to watch Tom enjoying his! After a few days Luke took me to one side. 'Are there any biscuits you could buy that look like Hobnobs and taste like Hobnobs but which aren't Hobnobs?' he said. That was the moment when he learned about sticking to a decision taken!

So often we make decisions which are right but after a while the lack of co-operation from others and the difficulty of it all makes us try to rationalise our way out of it. I remember a friend talking about marriage. He said that we commit ourselves to each other when we're so much in love, and then one day, we wake up and wonder what on earth we've done - and that's when the vows we've taken begin to count. Having made a vow, a 'formal' decision, we stick with it.

We're hoping that the Hobnobs lesson (which he didn't enjoy again until Easter Day!) will help form a constancy in Luke which will serve him well later on. After all, it's being constant in small things that helps us when major problems occur.

MISSED TURNINGS

Last summer I was asked to speak in Berkhamsted. It's not very far from home but for once I'd allowed plenty of time to get there - just as well as it turned out. I was really enjoying myself driving along on a most beautiful day; the wayside flowers were splashes of vibrant colours and I even saw a rabbit running alongside the road. I was so grateful to God for His creation - I appreciate it so much more now that I know the Creator! Anyway, I was chatting to him, and saying thank you, when I saw a sign to Wendover that shouldn't have been there. At least, it shouldn't have been there on the way to Berkhamsted! In fact, of course, the sign was right and I was wrong - I'd missed the turning about 10 minutes earlier!!

I drove along that road again today and remembered how quickly I'd turned and driven across country to reach my appointment. I wondered if I'd often missed turnings in my life? You see, I'd enjoyed being on the wrong road and God had certainly been with me in my error. Actually it was the wrong road because I was meant to be somewhere else. Mind you, once I knew it was wrong, I turned pretty quickly and prayed very hard and I did ask Him to forgive my stupidity and rescue me, yet again, from a problem of my own making! And in His graciousness, He did.

I've no doubt it'll happen again - I'll miss a turning and be on the wrong road, probably even enjoying myself! But I'm sure He'll always put up a sign-post to re-direct me - and I know that if I then turn to Him, He'll get me to the right place on time!

SEPARATION

I have a friend who doesn't believe in God. I have many friends in this position but I was chatting to Alan recently about it. He said that he didn't think he could come to God for insurance, as that wouldn't be a right reason. In human terms, of course, it wouldn't seem very honest to turn to God 'just in case' but as I thought about it I realised that the whole scenario changes when we consider the Fatherhood of God.

Our eldest son, Adam, is going round the world during this coming year, so there is going to be a time of separation for us. But what if, during his time away, something happened which made him unable to contact us, or, perhaps, he just didn't want to keep in touch any longer? As time passes it makes it more and more difficult to restore relationships so, perhaps, years and years pass and even if he changed his mind he might not be able to bring himself to heal the breach. Maybe, in twenty years, if we became very famous or rich (!) Adam would hear of it.

What if he then said, 'I can't contact them now - they'll think I'm only doing it because of what I'll get.'

And yet - how we'd have longed over the years for us to be reunited. How great our joy would be to be reconciled with him, whatever the reason. If we would feel like that in our imperfect, inadequate love - how can we begin to comprehend the longing of Our Father to be reunited with His children? And HIS JOY!

'He will rejoice over you with happy song. He will renew you by his love. He will dance with shouts of joy for you as on a day of festival.' *(Zephaniah 3:17)*

16

SUFFERING MISERABLY

In 1975 when the Lord lit His flame in me, I promised Him that I would never let it go out but that I would fan it so that others would see it and believe in Him as well. I was even rash enough to say that when I got old, really old, and began to suffer the aches and pains of ageing, I would be sure to suffer with joy - shining with His love so that people would know that it was His presence which ruled my life and gave me serenity and happiness.

Well, last week reality caught up with me in the form of aching shoulders -they hurt so much that I was unable to lift my arms up high enough to do my hair. And what happened? Did I shine with peace and joy? I'm afraid not. I was thoroughly unhappy - moaning to family and friends and failing miserably to function efficiently as wife and mum! It was amazing how easy it was to sink into the depths of self-pity and, for two days, I sunk!

I want to say that I think I've learnt my lesson. It is only going to be by God's Grace that I can shine and I need to be much closer to Him than I am so that His strength will be my strength. In the meantime I want to apologise to anyone who is in pain because I thought I could cope with anything and I've learnt that I can't. My admiration goes out to you - and my prayers for His blessings and His strength.

THE GREATEST SIGN

I'm getting pretty fed up with words and symbols being hi-jacked so that I feel guilty using them 'normally.' I am really sad that 'gay' now has such connotations that it is no longer acceptable in every-day parlance and I'm pretty cross that the New Age have adopted the rainbow as their logo. Rainbows have always been very special to me, so very mysterious and beautiful and, of course, a sign of the covenant God established with Noah and all life on earth. A sign of His everlasting love.

But the most exasperating thing just now is the way that people are always asking, 'What sign are you?' Not just non-believers but also Christians who should know better: Christians who read their horoscopes each day laughingly say, 'It's only a bit of fun!' and yet act and react later on. People say 'If you're such and such a sign then you're definitely a -' - and immediately you're in bondage to a pre-supposed characteristic.

Not me - I'm a new creation in the Lord and the only general characteristics I want to have are His. The list is comprehensive enough - love, joy, peace, patience, kindness, goodness, faithfulness, gentleness and self-control. I really can't think of anything else anyone could need or want to be.

So I've decided that in future when someone asks me what sign I am I will say - 'I'm the sign of the cross.' And if they say, 'What's that?' I shall have the greatest joy in telling them that it's the sign of a child of God - a follower of Christ. That it means He is the Son who rules my life and He has a plan for me which I can choose to follow for perfect peace.

I'm NOT having my life ruled by the stars and planets which, after all, were created through Him.

Come on, Christians - hands up everyone who's ruled by the SON!

THE MOUNTAIN OF THE LORD

Charles and I had the good fortune to spend Pentecost in Innsbruck this year at a conference. Because neither of us speak German we were helped by a brilliant translator, but it did mean we were careful in choosing the right words and phrases. Charles is used to this but I'm not, so during the Monday Mass, when I felt God had given me a picture for the conference, I turned to Charles to check it out and ensure that the words I used would be understood. It was during rather loud praise that I turned to him and said, 'I think the Lord has given me a picture - will you hear it through for me?

'I can see an alpine horn on the side of the mountain. It's very large indeed - much bigger than the people who are standing alongside about half way up it. The people think that they can stay where they are because when God speaks through it, they'll hear the echoes from the hills, but in fact, God isn't going to speak through it, instead He's going to pour things down it so they'll have to move to the mouthpiece to pick things up.

'I think it means that sometimes we try to anticipate what God is going to do next because He's following a familiar pattern, but He's saying not to restrict him with our expectations. We must be ready to 'move' to receive new things in new ways.'

I looked at Charles and he looked a little concerned. 'I think it's a bit complicated.' he said. 'A bit difficult - I'd hold onto it for now.'

'Fair enough.' I replied, and returned to praising God. However, as we went up to our room later, I came back to the picture. 'I do think it's really important, you know!' 'O.K,' he said, 'run it past me again.'

'Well,' I started, 'I have this picture of an alpine horn on the mountainside.' 'Alpine horn!' he exclaimed. 'I thought you said Albert Hall!' I looked at him blankly. 'Why would the Albert Hall be on the mountainside?' 'I told you I thought it was complicated,' he replied.

Next morning I shared the picture, the explanation and the misunderstanding with the conference - in God's perfect timing!!!

Come away, my love, and be like a gazelle or like
a young stag on the spice laden mountains.
Song of Songs 8:14

MORE DISCIPLINE !

Last summer was happily hectic with various conferences and family activities, and there was one week when I wasn't sure whether I was coming or going.

Charles was leaving for conference number one; Luke was leaving for America for four weeks, and as he was returning just before starting a new school, we had to buy all the new kit and 'name-tape' everything. End of term festivities were upon us with a vengeance; I owed Adam, in Australia, a letter and I really did not know which way to turn next.

The best way to describe it is that I felt that my mind was like a room full of very active 'needs' rushing around like a bunch of totally uncontrolled, boisterous children. Every so often I would open the door, grab the first 'need' rushing past, drag it out, slam the door and try to deal with it! The noise from my 'mind room' was constant and undiminishing. I think other 'needs' were continuously pouring in through the back door!

One day I'd had enough - things were getting out of control. I thought about this picture of the chaotic room. I sat down and pictured myself outside the door. The tumult from inside was quite unnerving. I flung open the door and screamed, 'STOP' and I pictured the 'needs' stopping dead in their tracks in amazement.

From the newly formed queue I beckoned the first 'need' to the door. 'Outside, you're next - and the rest of you wait quietly until I'm ready.'

I breathed a deep sigh, wrote a neat list and relaxed in my

peaceful mind. I examined the need and dealt with it before starting the next. That day I cleared 'the room' of most of the essential needs, realising that it was my own fault that things had got so bad.

Is there a spiritual lesson here? Well, I know that God only asks of me what He knows I can manage, so if I'm in a chaotic mess it can only be of my own making! Obviously a little more discipline in my life-style is called for. In future I shall endeavour to prioritise everything as it appears. Instead of waiting for the room to fill up - I shall do something about it straight away. Anyway, that's the theory!!

INNER CHILD

Recently I heard an excellent talk on inner healing. It was on the lines of the damaged child within each of us and how, as adults, we need to look back on our lives - to times when we've been hurt, intentionally or not - for Jesus to help us to forgive and then to heal those memories. She spoke of many people whose adult behaviour and attitudes had been formed by incidents long forgotten, and how prayer ministry has been the key to transformed lives.

Talks like this really make one sit up and take notice and, usually, change one's life because 'things happen' as we come before the Lord. But they also have another effect on me - they make me wonder how I'm doing as a parent. Am I causing unnecessary problems for our offspring? I must say that I do react differently now that I think of the long-term consequences.

Several years ago, Charles and I had been away for a few days and my father had been looking after Luke (6) and Tom (3). They always have a marvellous time when this happens and I don't think they miss us much at all! Anyway, we returned quite late and the following morning I got Tom ready for playschool. He decided that he would rather stay at home with me and so made a bit of a fuss. I insisted that, as he was well and I had lots to do, he would be fine once we got to school, but he really complained and started to cry when I tried to leave him. So in the end I gave in. On the way back to the car park we met a Christian friend.

'Oh, it's a day to be with Mummy, is it Tom?' She said.

He nodded.

'Actually,' I said, 'It's the thought of Tom in 40yrs time, sitting in a room for a time of ministry, saying - I remember a day when my mother forced me into playschool.... - I'm trying to save ministry time here!'

One small surrender for a son's happiness - not a lot to ask really.

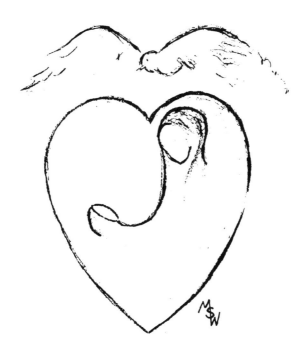

WE SAW HIS GLORY

On the 2nd Sunday after Christmas, we were sitting in a small West Country church listening to an excellent homily by a dear friend of ours, and the phrase from the Gospel on which we focused was: 'And we saw His glory.'

I've thought about it so much since then - how His glory is around us in so many simple ways and yet we miss it. I know that as a chid I had a sense of wonder about things, which has since dampened down - not just by growing older but also by the way 'everything is common-place'.

I mean - I loved going to see strange/unusual animals in zoos - but the nature programmes on TV means that they are now familiar and much better understood in their natural environment.   I remember the anticipation of Whitsun treats in Sunday School, holidays by the sea, trips to special places.   Life was full but there were lots of 'special things' which happened rarely, and in their rarity, they were exciting.   Like the first new potatoes, strawberries, tomatoes - I remember when they only appeared in season!

We are so blasé these days - every thing is so easy to do, to see, to have - and I find that this drifts over into the spiritual! I take so much for granted - even the glory of God.   This year, I'd like to help restore the wonder of God and His glory - to see Him resplendent in His creation and acts. To know and appreciate the glory of the Word made flesh - full of grace and truth.

Father finished his homily with a joke which reminds me, when I think of it, of how we can miss His glory if we look with the eyes of the world.

A man loved hunting and had a new hunting dog. On the first day of the hunting season they set out and he started shooting ducks as they flew over a lake. When the first one fell into the water he sent the dog out to pick it up, and to his amazement the dog walked across the water! It happened again and again. The man got very excited and decided to invite his neighbour to join him on the following day. They set off to the same lake - shot a duck - duck in water - dog walks across water to retrieve duck. This continued all day but the neighbour said nothing. Towards evening the man couldn't wait any longer. 'Do you notice anything strange about my dog?' He asked. 'Well,' said the neighbour, 'I haven't liked to say anything but, do you know - your dog can't swim!'

DARE WE STEP OUT IN FAITH?

Luke had a bit of a problem last week. Mother's Day loomed and the time for purchasing a gift had come. He came to me with the sad statement that he did not have any money. I'd heard him discussing another purchase with Tom only a few days earlier and when I asked him about that, he replied, 'I haven't any money because I'm saving up for a computer game.'

It was quite hard to explain that he did have money but he was allocating it to a future plan and not an immediate need. In his mind, the money in the box was for a specific purpose and could not possibly be used for something else.

It is very easy to compartmentalise our lives so that there is little overlap - particularly with spiritual gifts which we receive so freely from God, yet tend to restrict to our Christian meetings and friends. I don't know how many times I've listened to a tale of woe from an acquaintance - about illness or difficult circumstance - and wondered what on earth I could do to help, when maybe, the day before I'd been happily praying for healing etc. in the prayer group. I wonder why we try to pigeonhole everything - to keep thoughts, actions and ideas in neat boxes all labelled for appropriate times and places. Maybe we like to keep control, or maybe we're scared that we'll open ourselves to misunderstanding and ridicule.

I've heard wonderful testimonies from people who've spoken to complete strangers in response to God's prompting. They didn't hesitate to use what they had and trust God for the follow up. Someone was describing how she sat behind such a person on a platform listening to his latest 'foray for God' and asking God why he was used in such a spectacular way.

'Because he's not afraid to get egg on his face' was the reply!

Maybe we should use what we have and not save it for the future need - and carry plenty of tissues for the egg on the face!

The Lord's 'phone - Fatima '97

Call unto me and I will answer you
Jer. 33:3

THOUGHTFUL GIVING

Recently I overheard Luke and Tom negotiating a rise in their pocket money. At least, Luke was negotiating as, at 13yrs old, he understands the increase in the cost of his 'necessities' pretty well. I could hear that 'everything has gone up' and 'I need more,' and I was chuckling to myself as I remembered having similar discussions with my own father.

Suddenly I felt God say 'What about me?'

I was a bit confused as my initial reaction was that I don't give Him pocket money and, of course, as a family we tithe from our income. But I realised He meant my additional personal offerings to Him when I am at a Christian meeting or service and the plate comes round.

When I first started giving in 1976 I gave £1 which, I thought, was a very fair and generous amount, but I'm still giving £1 seventeen years later. I'm not saying that £1 is not a generous offering - indeed, for some people it's more than they can manage - but, for me, I've never really thought of 'upping the gifts' and the Lord drew my attention to it in the nicest possible way!

I don't think he wants me to swing the other way and cause financial problems with the housekeeping because of an 'excessive offering' made from a guilty conscience. I'll have to think about it and ask the Lord what I should be giving. I might even look up the notes I made once about 'Revelation Giving' - it could be time to put them into practice.

PLAN WELL AND ACCEPT CHANGE

We've just recently enjoyed our Prayer Group Barbecue - a joint effort by all on food and the gift of a dry day from God! Actually the dry day looked extremely doubtful at 11.30 am with folks due to arrive eat at 12.00 noon, but prayer, faith and the grace of God triumphed and the sun managed to shine until 5.00 pm just after the last person left. That was one occasion when the plans we'd made actually came to fruition in the manner hoped for. But I've been thinking a lot lately about the other times - when plans carefully laid, expectations held and blessings claimed have come to nought.

When Charles and I got engaged we made lots of plans - very detailed ones - and we enjoyed every minute of the planning. My mother once said, 'You spend so much time planning - I hope you won't be disappointed if it all goes wrong - if it all proves to be a waste of time!'

I tried to explain that even if everything changed, the planning was half the fun anyway and we knew that the goal had to be held lightly because we had to live in the reality of life, not in our ideal.

Being Christian means we try to plan our lives within God's will - to His plan - but being human, our discernment of His will is not perfect. This means that what we hope and work for does not always come about - and how should we act then? I think we have to take a deep breath and get on with living the life we have - accepting the circumstances over which we have no control and no possibility of changing. That's not being defeated but being victorious - after all it's only by the strength of Christ that we accept with joy what we have if it's not what we'd choose.

Did you know that there are two ways to be content? One way is to have all you want - the other is to be content with what you have.

I'm not saying that we stop striving for change, praying for healing or expecting miracles, but I think the time comes when reality must be faced and it becomes necessary to say - 'Your will, not mine, Lord. Please give me the strength and joy to live my life as it is.'

Father, into your hands I commit my Spirit.
Belfast October '93

TURNING TO THE SON-LIGHT

Charles and I have just returned from Italy where we were privileged to share in a retreat at Assisi. We met in the Tent of Unity, which had been erected at the top of a very steep hill so each day we really felt like pilgrims climbing to be with God. I'm not saying we found the climb easy - I was very impressed by those who managed to walk and talk as they journeyed up - but I think it was made easier for each of us knowing that God was calling us by name to spend time with Him.

One beautiful morning a friend and I stood looking out across the plain. The sun was shining strongly and we longed to praise this wonderful God of ours who had been giving us so much - challenging teaching, quiet times in His presence and Love, so much Love. As we poured out our hearts to Him in thanksgiving I found myself turning to face the sun - to feel its warmth even more fully on my face - and I felt the Father say, 'How can you feel the fullness of my Son's glory if you do not turn into the Son-light?'

I realised that the place where we should be is before His throne, adoring Him - looking full into His wonderful face.

We need not fear that we will neglect the world by doing this - so often we try to concentrate on solving problems, just glancing back over our shoulders to praise Him. But if we look into His face and glory, any worldly problem will come as a cloud between us and we will instantly be aware of the shadow - and then He will guide our thoughts and prayers, and lead us into necessary action.

As we basked in the sun, enjoying the warmth - revelling in the presence of His Son, feeling His joy well up inside us - I wondered why we make our relationship with Him so very complicated.

Fr Cantalamessa, who was our retreat master, had reminded us again that the Law of the Spirit is Love - OUR GOD IS LOVE.

May we be so aware of being loved by Him and so determined to love Him, that His love flows through us to others, effortlessly. *(Romans 13:10.)*

The Father Heart of God

BECAUSE OF JESUS

For the past three years I have had the privilege of walking a friend's dog most mornings. She has three beautiful golden retrievers so, after dropping the boys off at school, Di, Anne and I go for a brisk, slightly frenetic 3 mile walk for one hour – depending on the weather. We have such fun! Because we walk the same route every day, some people wonder what we find to talk about. I don't know really, but I should think we've covered most subjects by now. I do know that we laugh a lot – get tangled up with dogs' leads, trees and each other and, at the end, feel 100% better. Sometimes, in the rain, we think we must be mad, but if we can we walk because we enjoy it so much – the exercise and the company.

Recently we were walking an hour later than usual and it was surprising how many people we met coming out of their houses who said, 'You're late today' – and one gentleman greeted us with – 'Oh, the ladies who walk!' Other people tell us that they see us most mornings and wonder how we can always be so happy. It made me realise that as we go through life, many people's eyes are on us that we know nothing about. They see how we behave – how we look, react to things. They wonder about our lives – what makes us tick.

Doesn't that sound exciting yet daunting? It means to me that we really are the Lord's 'letters ... known and read by all men.' (2 Cor.3:2. RSV). Many years ago I used to see Fiona Castle at our daughter's school – always smiling, looking very happy. When we became friends, I told her how I'd always wondered about that and she said – 'it's because of Jesus.' May all our lives be a silent witness to those who see us – because of Jesus.

HEART CLEANSING

When I was asked to write for this month's magazine, I must confess that my immediate reaction was that I couldn't possibly - not on heart cleansing! I think that I reacted like that because when writing an article, I have to look at myself more closely and all those 'nasty bits' that I've tried to ignore come rushing into focus, demanding to be addressed. The breakthrough came when I sat down one day after a 'serious discussion' with my teenage sons about dirty washing. Why is it that sons seem unable to co-operate in the civilised routine of recycling dirty clothes? They know that if they bring them to me I will happily wash them, iron them and return them in perfect condition to be worn again. But somehow, they don't think - they leave them around in their rooms until I go and find them. As I sat with my cup of coffee, meditating on the complex relationships involved in being a parent, I felt a little nudging from the Lord.

'Why is it,' He said, 'that you have areas in your life which I could heal, clean up and restore for you, and you never bring them to me? Why do I have to prompt you over and over again when you know how much I love you and long to make things 'right' for you?'

What could I say? Time, I think, to put pen to paper and seriously consider what heart cleansing truly means to us.

Firstly, I think, we need to know that only God can cleanse our hearts. We cannot do that - we can only desire that it is done and be willing to surrender to it. In Mark 7, Jesus accuses the Pharisees of being hypocrites; of thinking that ritual cleansing made them acceptable to God. But He knew that their worship was motivated, not by love, but by those hidden agendas of profit, prestige and status - are we always innocent of those charges? We are not pure because of our outward acts - we become pure on the inside as Christ renews our mind and transforms us.

'For out of the overflow of his heart his mouth speaks.' *Luke 7: 45*

What practical steps can we decide to take so that this transformation can happen?

1 Already said - our righteousness comes from what God does in us, not from what we can do by ourselves.
2 We must be God-centred, not self-centred.
3 Our righteousness is based on reverence for God and not on approval by other people.
4 Our righteousness goes beyond keeping the Law to living the principles behind the Law.

And the major principle behind God's Law is LOVE. It's not enough to clean up our actions and words - we need to allow the Holy Spirit to fill us with new attitudes - we need to let His Love be the source of all we say and do - in all things and at all times. Easier said than done, I fear - 'at all times' is pretty all-embracing! But following God half-heartedly is not really good enough, is it? And He's not asking us to do anything we cannot do - because even as we decide to do it, so He equips us with all we need, not to fail! No matter how long we have been following Christ, no matter what status we have in our spiritual walk, we must still depend on God for our spiritual vitality.

And our hearts? In the natural, physical sense, our hearts are pumps which circulate 'life-giving' blood around the body. They 'take in' and they 'give out' constantly. I want to take in Love from my Father - a never ending source - and I want to give it out to those around me.

I don't know about you, but I'm going to have a major spring clean and collect up all my dirty washing for my Father!

'Create in me a pure heart, O Lord, and renew a steadfast spirit in me. *Psalm 51*

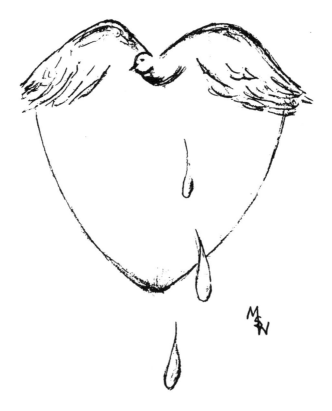

Create in me a New Heart

MOST PRECIOUS CHILD

It's funny how our 'role in life' changes. We start off as 'children' but move into 'grown-ups' when we meet responsibilities either through relationships, work or even having children of our own. I remember how very 'grown-up' I felt when Lucy and Adam were very small and dependent on us and yet, whenever we went to visit my parents, I slipped very easily into the 'child' role again. My mother would take over the responsibility of providing food, entertaining the children - and there was always a concern for me, her child, which was somehow different to that caring which Charles had.

My mother died over 12 years ago and I remember vividly the time I went back to visit my father some months later. I wasn't feeling too well and so after unpacking and settling the children, Charles sent me to bed - and I suddenly realised that I had no mother 'above' me - I was 'top of the tree' so to speak. I longed, so very much, to be a child again with my mum.

This week I watched a young couple with their new baby and saw how they had moved into a new responsible position. But I saw too that they would occasionally long to be 'the child' again - to have a parent to run to who would let them be children - dependent. And that is what our heavenly father promises us. He says that we will always be His children - that we will never reach the 'top of the tree' with Him - safe in His love, relaxing in our dependence on Him, secure in the knowledge that, to Him, we will always be ...

His most precious child.

HUNGRY FOR GOD'S WORD

Isn't it interesting how some of God's rules are so different from the natural ones? For example - the more of His love we give away, the more we seem to have! That always surprises me. Usually, if we pour water out of a full jug, the level immediately goes down. But with the Living Spirit water, the more it flows out - the more remains within us. By nature we want to hold onto good things - to keep them for ourselves. But if we want to keep God's love, we just have to keep giving it away.

When I first came into this wonderful personal relationship with Jesus, I thought I knew everything (I was very presumptuous and rather obnoxious!). I thought I knew all about Him but the more I learnt, the less I seemed to know and the more there was to learn. It's wonderful to think that there'll always be something new to learn about Him, that I'll never have enough knowledge of Him - even if I devoted every moment to finding out. It seems that as my knowledge of Him grows, my ignorance increases.

This train of thought started because I recently heard someone say 'If we stop reading scripture, we stop being hungry for scripture.' Normally, if we're hungry and eat, the hunger goes; but with scripture, the more we try to assuage that hunger, the more hungry we become. And it IS true - if we do NOT read the Bible, the desire to do so fades.

The lesson for me? If I can get through a day without reading His word and not feel something missing - I've got a problem! *The answer for me?* Don't wait until I LONG to read - make a decision to do so and get on with it! I know now that once I start, the hunger will come back.

STARTING THE DAY RIGHT

Tom couldn't wait until his friend got out of the car one day after school. 'I've got something to tell you, Mum - I kicked a boy in school today.' I was amazed. Tom is not the lashing out kind and is not, generally speaking, into fighting of any description. He's definitely not one of the heavy brigade.

'What happened?' I asked.

'Well, he's been getting at me all week when we play football - being silly, mucking about and ruining the game.' (This is a cardinal sin in the eyes of an 11yr old) 'I was just running up the playground, dribbling the ball, - I'd got past all my friends - when he came in and kicked it away - he wasn't even playing - and I was so cross that something inside me snapped and I kicked him on the shin. I said I was sorry immediately but a teacher had seen me and sent me inside.'

I took a deep breath. Was this a new trend? I thought not. 'What then?'

'Well, Mrs B (his teacher) was very surprised and said it wasn't like me at all and I couldn't explain why it had happened. Something just came over me.' He was very upset and truly sorry so I didn't feel a heavy reprimand from me was needed.

'I hope that's the first and last time it happens.' I said. 'By the way, are you still doing your Bible study in the morning?' 'Not this week.' he said. 'I've been a bit rushed.'

'Well there you are then!' I intoned righteously. 'When we spend time with Jesus in the morning it sort of sets the day right for us. When we read the Bible we grow more and more like Him and then when people make us cross we don't react in a temper and hit them or shout at them.'

'Oh!' he said immediately, 'You didn't do your Bible study yesterday then, when you shouted at Luke and me?'

Out of the mouths of babes ....

9th Nov. '95

PASSING TIME

I really cannot believe how fast time flies by these days. I know that it's partly because I'm older - my mother always used to say the same thing when I was little and I could never understand her then - but it really is as if someone has pressed a fast-forward button, and if I blink I miss a day.

It's made me think quite a lot lately about TIME, because the same length of time can feel totally different depending on whether or not I'm enjoying it. For example: I sat and prayed with someone who rested in the Spirit for an hour and it felt like 10 minutes, and I've listened to a 10 minute talk that felt like an hour! Sometimes it's helpful when something horrid is happening to think 'This too will pass' but trying to understand time is usually confusing. And what about in heaven? Will that be for a 'long time'? or will we all be having such a 'good time' that 'no time' passes at all?

Recently I read some Bible Study Notes in New Daylight. Gerard W. Hughes was writing about God in the present moment. 'Time does not exist in itself, it is a measure of change. If we were not conscious of change, we would have no concept of time'.

This helps explain how I think about heaven. I think we will be so absorbed in the unchanging God who will be with us and who we will be worshipping in glory, that the 'long time' will be 'no time'. But it doesn't help explain the here and now, where it's as if so much is changing that time can't keep up. I've decided to stop worrying about it and follow the rest of Gerard's advice.

'God lives always in the now. One way of developing this consciousness is to practise living in the present. As St. Augustine said: 'Do whatever you are doing,' so if you are washing the dishes, wash the dishes and don't be planning what you are going to do when you have finished.'

So now I've finished this article - what next?

Collect Tom; Luke to dentist; get ready for prayer group; cook supper; I wonder what Charles would say if I tell him he shouldn't be booking things in for the year after next?

I can see this is not going to be as easy as I thought!

TRIALS

It was our annual prayer group BBQ and Charles, as chief chef, had volunteered to purchase the meat; so he set out for the freezer shop on Saturday morning. He found the right car park and cleverly parked next to the lift on the first floor. Buying frozen meat is not as easy as some people think: It entails checking that each packet contains the requisite number of pieces and working out the unit cost - so it was quite a while before he left with a supermarket trolley loaded down. Then the fun began - the lift was broken.

There was much consternation amongst the waiting shoppers until someone suggested the other lift on the far side of the precinct. Arriving there, Charles found a very large crowd waiting so it was 15 minutes before he got into the lift which then proceeded to the 2nd floor, refusing to stop at the 1st! Charles got out to consider the next move. Perhaps he could walk down the car ramp? The cars were travelling down in a steady stream so this did not seem an attractive proposition, but while thinking about it one of the wheels fell off the trolley! Wheeling the unbalanced rogue machine back towards the lift, he saw that the first lift now appeared to be functioning, so he crossed the car park with some difficulty, got into the lift, pressed the button for the 1st floor and found himself on the ground floor once more, facing a huge crowd waiting to get in! With profound apologies to those who joined him in the lift, he returned to the 2nd floor. A quick check on the staircase confirmed that it was much too steep for the trolley, so he paused to review the situation.

A lady had been sitting in her car watching his various manoeuvres, and couldn't keep silent any longer. 'You're not having a very good day, are you?' she enquired kindly. 'Are you lost, or have you lost your car?' 'No' replied Charles. 'I know where I am, and I know where my car is, but I can't get to it!'

Fortunately the lift arrived back at that moment and the man who got out assured Charles that the lift was now stopping at the 1st floor - which it did.

I listened to my husband's story on his return, highly amused by the pictures it conjured up. This man I love, who is so organised, had had to cope with such a frustrating and unpredictable morning.

'What did you learn from all that?' I said. 'Patience,' he replied. 'A lot of patience - and to smile at people when they make inane comments.'

Isn't God good, and hasn't He got a sense of humour!

PRIORITISING MY TIME

It's just a few weeks to Christmas as I write this, but I know that it will be January before you read it! I just want to say that I will not be pressured into panicking about 'getting everything ready.'

There are members of my family who finished their Christmas shopping nearly a month ago and have, no doubt, already written their cards, possibly sent them! I am delighted that they are so organised - but I have neither bought nor written a card as yet.

Christmas should be a time of peace, tranquillity and love; of drawing closer to Jesus, recognising his willingness to become vulnerable and in receiving his gift of love, looking around us to see who we can share it with. I will not let the expectations of the world spoil that.

I've decided not to worry, and I've worked out a general principle to help! Basically I'm learning to prioritise my time. Whenever I feel guilty about not doing something I focus on it and ask - 'Do I do it now or not?' If I feel I should do it, I do it - if not, it's usually because there's something more important to do, and I do that. That means that I can't feel guilty over the first thing, because it wasn't the top priority.

I've been trying it for a while now and it's really working. I had two talks to prepare, a few letters, this article, the school library to organise, children's Christmas shows, football matches, ironing, meetings, Christmas shopping, cards etc.., etc.. an infinite variety of activities. Anyway, each day something else came to the top of the priority list and things were done in time (Christmas activities are creeping up - nearer the top on this week's list!). I found that

I wasted less time, as I realised there were deadlines and fixed appointments. I certainly watched less TV (no bad thing!) and I didn't manage any embroidery (but that can wait until the New Year).

Christmas is going to be great again this year. We will relax, talk, play games, sing 'Happy Birthday' to Jesus and not panic. I've one more talk before Christmas - 'Peace amongst pressure?' - His peace, of course. Just thinking of it makes one feel better. I'm so very glad that his peace is not dependent on circumstances but on his presence within our hearts. That talk can wait a few days, so the next priority is overseas cards!!

ALL IN A NAME

It all started because Tom is being confirmed this year and needed to choose his confirmation name. His choice is Samuel - because, as he said, 'When God called him, he heard him and said 'Yes'.' I wonder if any of us could have given such a decisive reason for choosing a name?

Some people like their given names very much, and if they are biblical, like Peter, they often feel identification with the well-known character. But to choose an extra name - it made me think and chat to friends; to ask them what their choice would be for themselves. It was most interesting!

Jonathan - he was a true friend and when the sign he asked for from God happened, he acted on it with confidence.

Barnabas - always encouraging people to move on with God.

There's *Jeremiah*, who was not afraid to tell people what God was saying.

Enoch , who walked with God until he 'was not'!

And *Caleb* who, with Joshua, had a different spirit to the rest of his people.

For the ladies there's *Ruth* - willing to forsake everything for the truth she found.

Abigail - beautiful and wise, married to a most difficult and unpleasant man, who endured all and found happiness.

Lois - a 'housewife' who taught Eunice, her daughter (married to an unbeliever) and grandson, Timothy, all about Jesus.

And, of course, *Mary*, whose attributes are too numerous to mention.

I found a book we had bought many years ago - 'Who's Who in the Old Testament' - so many now unfamiliar names. Do you remember *Beno, Ithamar* and *Zaza*?

Tom suggested Charles should take *Luke* - because he wrote the word of God!!

Me? I think that I would opt for *Esther* because she was the right person in the right place at the right time and she was not afraid to stand up for her people.

It's been a fascinating and stimulating exercise - not yet finished, I suspect!

GOD'S COLOURS

Last week in church, I was challenged to remember my confirmation day, and the 'white veil' which I wore. The 'white' being God's colour - to symbolise my closeness to him. And I found myself thinking again of how wonderful colour is.

The rainbow, symbol of God's faithfulness, is white split into a myriad hues as if white holds all the other colours within itself - just as God is the only true 'completeness' that there is. We take colour so much for granted: a fact brought home to me once while I watched a film of a young boy deciding to show his blind girlfriend what colour is.

He sat her down and put in her hands a very hot stone. 'That's red,' he said, and as it cooled a little, 'Now it's pink.' And then he gave her an ice cube and said 'That's blue.' 'I see,' she said softly as the concept of colours began to take shape in her mind.

I wonder about God and all His Glory, and I think that our minds have no real concept of how wonderful and brilliant it is. Maybe there is another 'colour' beyond, which can mean nothing to us because 'we are blind.' But maybe, sometimes, He puts something or someone in our lives and we get a hint of what is to be. And in moments like that we too might say - hesitatingly, dubiously, no doubt joyously - 'I see.'

INNER DISABILITIES

I recently attended the funeral of our friend, Ian - a man we'd known for many years who, with his wife Pat, had moved from our area some time ago and I'm ashamed to say our communications had dwindled to little more than a Christmas letter. I say ashamed deliberately as, sitting in the church, memories of Pat and Ian came flooding back and I realised that I had learnt many things through their friendship - many lessons from the Lord. They had travelled quite a lot, last year to Israel, and many of the friends who had travelled with them came to the service. It was a true offering of praise in gratitude for a life well-lived.

So many anecdotes of love, humour and vitality - such a full life and yet, in the world's eyes, one of many problems, major difficulties. Ian suffered with cerebral palsy, as does Pat, and yet - as was said that day - his abilities far outweighed his disabilities. His ability to laugh and joke, to cause laughter around himself, was immense. His loyalty to family and friends unshakeable and his love for Pat totally protective and yet non-restrictive. His patience with others, especially when trying to make them understand him, seemed unending - as was his determination to correct injustice and discrimination. He was also bossy, stubborn and single-minded, but his only major regret I remember hearing about was that he couldn't have a car - the electric wheelchair was a poor substitute!

What did I learn from him? - how to be gracious in accepting help when necessary but not to be patronised. How humour can turn a potentially embarrassing situation into something amusing. How to accept other people's insensitivity without bitterness. How words are important, but communication needs talking and listening. How even the impossible becomes possible with determination and God's help. But God showed me a very important thing one day while praying with Pat and Ian for healing. When someone is physically ill or visibly handicapped, it's easier to formulate a prayer for healing - there's a ready-made focus, an easy target, if you like; but God sees the inner person - the personality as it were - and that is where the greater need often is, hidden behind the obvious. And for able-bodied people, we sometimes relax, thinking that we have no need for healing and yet our 'insides' are actually seriously disabled - but these disabilities are not permanent, the Lord longs to heal and transform them.

Just now we are praying for Pat for physical healing as she is really very poorly, but I suspect in the Lord's eyes, I might well need the greater healing miracle, and I do so want to be a person so transformed by the Lord that my abilities outweigh my disabilities.

FREE CHOICE

Do you ever feel that there's too much choice these days? Shopping in the supermarket is bewildering in the extreme. I remember when it was so much easier - only two brands of butter, one of sugar and not umpteen different cereals (each preferred by different members of the family!) And clothes - what a selection greets our eyes! Not just the variety of styles but the range of colours. When I was growing up it was navy, brown or bottle green and, possibly, a white cardigan for Sunday! I'm not really complaining - I love having the freedom to try different things and I really wouldn't like to return to the austerity days - it's just that choice can be confusing and sometimes I'd like not having to make it.

I was helping in the school library one Friday afternoon and this plaintive cry echoed up the corridor from the 6 year olds classroom - 'I don't want free choice' - and I knew exactly what he meant. Given 'free choice' we have to make decisions, and they may be right or wrong, but children have to be encouraged to make decisions in order to grow. First of all they learn the rules, follow the examples, then start making choices, and if they've learnt correctly they'll stay within the right framework.

So, the Good Lord gave us free will - the freedom to make choices. He gives us the rules (the Bible), the example of Jesus, and if we learn correctly we'll stay within His framework. Life choices are not like shopping, where what's relevant today is irrelevant or unimportant tomorrow. Life choices may seem large or small, but with each one we learn more about the Lord's will for us. And the great comfort for me, is that if I've prayed for guidance and my desire is to do His will, then the Lord will still be with me even if I've made the wrong choice. Growing up is hard and shouldering responsibility is not always easy, but to hear the Lord more clearly and to follow His way more closely is, I trust, the choice of us all. Because I know already that I will make mistakes, I'm so glad He loves me unconditionally!

I will refresh you

THE POWER OF GOD

Charles and I recently made a memorable journey; we visited Niagara Falls, and it really was an unforgettable experience.

It was a *very* hot day and the bus from the hotel had no air-conditioning, so by the time we reached the Falls we were very hot indeed. The boat trip on 'The Maid of the Mist' had an added attraction - not just to see the Falls close up but also to have the refreshing mist fall on us. As we waited to board the boat, we could see the Falls in the distance and we were given blue plastic hooded capes to wear. I hesitated to put mine on as I thought how pleasantly cool it would be to be wrapped in the mist, but when we boarded 'The Maid' it was pretty wet underfoot so I put on the cape and discovered that it nearly reached the floor - but I left my head uncovered.

The boat cast off and we started towards the Falls. Quite soon we began to feel their influence and, believe me, 'mist' is a misnomer! The spray was like light rain -I had my hood up *very* quickly - and then enjoyed the rain on my face. But the rain became more forceful and was soon cascading over us and I understood why the capes nearly reached the floor. The boat found it quite hard to go against the current but kept pushing on until it finally held it's position close-up to the Falls themselves.

I had turned away as the 'mist' was quite overpowering but in that moment of stillness, as the boat stopped, I turned and was overwhelmed by the power of the Falls. It was awe-inspiring. The water creamy white in it's falling, the thunderous roar and the forceful spray - and in that moment I caught a glimpse of the power of God, and I knew it was too much for me.

The boat turned and was propelled away at high speed by the force of the water and I suddenly realised that what I'd experienced spoke to me in quite a challenging way.

So often we sing 'Send thy power, O Lord' - but we have no idea what we are asking. We really have no concept of the power of God. Sometimes we come into the edge - the mist/spray - and even that is almost too much, in fact I'd tried to protect myself to lessen the effect. The boat had kept 'pushing in' towards the power, just as we are encouraged to draw closer to God. It had taken a lot of effort - and yet, at that moment of confrontation there had been a stillness in which nothing else had mattered - every ounce of my being had been focused on wonderful awesome power.

...I will pour out my Spirit in those days
Joel 2:29

HE LOVES US TO PIECES

Sr Mary Peter, Winifride, Sr Marian, Kristina, Anne, Erika, Viv, David and Charles invited Richard, Gio and I (the other halves!) to join them for a belated Christmas party last week. The National Service Committee Ensemble - talented, varied and extremely valuable. We met in Kristina's flat and enjoyed a great time of prayer and praise before a lovely meal.

It was fascinating to have time to talk and share memories. Sr Mary Peter and Winifride could remember starting the office nearly 20yrs ago (in their youthful 60's) - two ladies determined to serve the Renewal in a small office, sending out tapes and books and answering people's enquiries. Gradually the work grew and developed but the same servant hearts are evident in those who work there now. A slightly larger office with more books and tapes (Viv's Emporium) and an expanded/professional GOODNEWS, but the same desire among the staff to help.

The word that Sr Mary Peter had for us during the prayer time was that God wanted to meet us just where we were - and I want everyone to hear this! We so often think that we need to get things right; get things sorted; to change for the better or to stop being ...., before we can *really* expect God to have anything to do with us. Isn't it wonderful to know that whatever we're like, however we behave, He still 'loves us to pieces' (that's a quote from Cardinal Hume when he spoke to the young people at our ecumenical mission). I know it is not an excuse for a nasty nature or bad behaviour, but I am *so* glad our God loves us so.

And it's when we're sure of that fact, that we can care for others in a new way - loving with the Lord's love. I looked around the table on Saturday and I saw faces which glowed with the love of God. I saw people who God loved and with whom He was well pleased. And I felt privileged to be with them.

Our God

LIVING COLOURS

I have a new jacket - very bright! I bought it from a Christian charity - Toybox - which raises money for work among the street children of Guatemala. And it is *bright!* It is the sort of jacket which means that Charles will never lose me in a crowd - the sort which prompts complete strangers to talk to me - the sort which makes me smile every time I see it hanging in the hall. It brings such sunshine into the house with it's dazzling, unusual combination of colours. I think that Joseph's coat of many colours must have been similar - an early South American export!

Anyway, it's made me realise just how sombre a lot of the clothes are these days. I know that it is very 'uncool' to wear anything but black, grey or beige but I do wonder *why* this attitude is so prevalent amongst us. It's almost as if the world's hardness, depression, lethargy and lack of hope are being expressed visibly for all to see. And even though the cry of youth is 'we are all individuals' there seems to be a desire to melt into the crowd - no way should 'I' be different.

And that is sad. After the war (the 2nd World War, I hasten to add!) I remember money being short, but there was hope in abundance. We all had amazingly individual clothes, mostly because they had to be made, and our sweaters were a riot of colour because Mum knitted them - Fairisle patterns to use up all the bits of wool which she had. I'm not suggesting that it would be good to go back to those days, but maybe it would be nice to think about telling the world that WE ARE HAPPY by expressing our joy and happiness in the Lord in our appearance. What an impact we could have - radiant smiles above living colours!

Bright colours make people smile; make people 'lighten up'. Remember that the first rainbow came after a very stormy, black time. In the past on a 'grey day', I've felt as if I had a rainbow inside me trying to burst out, because of the joy and love of Christ's presence within. It's wonderful, now, to put on a 'rainbow' to go out.

I thoroughly recommend it to everyone!!!

CALLED BY NAME

At last, Charles and I have joined the Grandparents Club - along with Jan & Patrick Knight and Viv (now 'Granny Viv' of Books & Tapes) & Richard Sewell!! We are all inordinately proud and will no doubt bore you with our photographs given the slightest opportunity.

Anyway, last year I was writing about 'names' and I thought that I could continue that theme. Our daughter , Lucy , and her husband, Martin, invited me to go with them to see the baby on a scan - what a privilege to see this new creation before birth. During the scan the nurse asked if they had chosen names for the babe.

'Only for a girl' they said.
'You want to do what we did' said the nurse.
'When my daughter was born I asked the doctor if he had a daughter and he said, yes - Fiona - so we called our daughter, Fiona. Just as well she wasn't a boy as the doctor's name was Aeneas!'

As we were walking back to the car, Martin said 'I like that - if it's a boy we'll call him Eli.'
'Eli, why Eli?!' Lucy and I choroused.
'Well, like that nurse said'
'She never said 'Eli' - she said 'Aeneas'.'
'No, I don't like that - but I do like Eli.'
And that was that. With no knowledge of the biblical connection, Martin chose their son's name.

For a few months there was much discussion over such an unusual name and during a family party at Christmas, Tom said 'Why not call him 'Eliott' - it's quite like Eli.'

And so, that's his name - Eliott. But would you believe it - we later discovered that Eliott is Scottish for Eli and Eli means exalted or uplifted. Having thought about the importance of our names before, it's very interesting that this little one has been called 'by name' in such a definite and unexpected way.

Watching children grow up is always exciting - and I'm sure that Eliott, Hannah Sewell and John Knight will bring us a lot of joy and challenge in the years to come.

May the Lord bless them and may each of them find, and walk, the path which their heavenly father has already prepared for them to walk in.

Make me a channel of your peace

INFORMED FAITH

Like many other parents, we have just lived through school exams, again. Luke is an old hand at the game - he was sitting his GCSE's this year - but Tom was taking 'subject' exams for the first time. Both of them were very good over their revision - they drew up revision timetables and managed to cover the work as they'd planned - so we were interested to hear Tom's reaction to his first paper - History.

'How did it go?' we asked. 'Oh, it was O.K' he replied. 'The thing is, I needn't have bothered to do so much revision - they were only interested in what I thought.'

I think that is a *classic* reply! Forget the facts - what do I think? Forget the teaching, the research, the projects - it's what 'I think' that matters. On that basis we can all be experts in all fields due to our ability to express our thoughts. I don't think so!!

And yet, how many of us have informed minds when it comes to our beliefs? How many of us think it enough to say 'Well, I think......' What about the church's teachings and, above all, the Scriptures? Are we truly conversant with them? Are we able to substantiate our thoughts with facts and examples? Can we quote scripture and verse to validate our arguments? Speaking for myself - I think not!

So, finding Tom's answer amusing has made me realise how easy it is to be complacent in my faith. All I know is that I don't know enough, and never will! That must be a good starting point for improvement.

PEARLS

Sometimes writing this column is extremely difficult! This one is a case in point. It started off quite well -

Charles and I celebrated our 30th wedding anniversary in September. Most people sent us cards with pearls on and my sister even found a glass oyster with a pearl inside. We had a lovely family celebration and our children gave us photographs of themselves (including Eliott) which they had had taken a few weeks previously.

I was looking at the photos and I suddenly thought of what very appropriate presents they were. After all, our children *are* pearls to us, each and every one of them. A few days later I took the imagery a little further. Each pearl grows because something irritating is covered in something beautiful. (It's a good thing I didn't stop there because that is not a helpful picture of our children!) But each natural pearl grows into a uniquely beautiful object - a much better picture!

My next thought was 'Am I a pearl of God's?' and this is when the column became difficult to write because the analogy falls apart! Pearls start because a bit of grit gets into an oyster and in order to tolerate it, the oyster secretes something beautiful around it - for its own comfort. But God isn't like that. He never sees us as an irritant which must be tolerated. We are already beautiful in God's sight.

So do I forget about this or is it just that I am trying to draw the wrong conclusion? I really felt that God was trying to say something and suddenly I thought about human relationships.

Those certainly involve irritation and need tolerance.   To go back to our children; have I allowed the Lord to use me as a loving covering around them to enable his beauty and glory to grow?   How about the rest of my family and friends?   God willing, between us all we could have a beautiful necklace of pearls made out of our relationships, grown in tolerance and love.

I will draw all men unto me ....

BLESSED BY LIFE

I was recently reminded of a Presbyterian minister, Nantlais Williams, who taught at Sunday School during my teenage years. Looking back now I realise that he was an anointed preacher (I've just discovered that his father was an evangelist during the Welsh Revival) and I am grateful for his influence on my life.

One Sunday in 1959, as he preached, he held up a little book and said that it was his 'personal memories'. He encouraged us to buy a book and write down any quotes, poems or scriptures which made us think or which we especially liked. I started my book that week and it really is precious to me. Many of the writings are not overtly Christian but I like to think that some of them have been written into my subconscious. Interestingly there are also many Christian thoughts which I wrote down during my atheistic 12yrs - God was obviously trying to talk to me even then! Here are some which you might like:

There are two ways to be rich. One is to have everything you want; the other is to be content with what you have.

Better to remain silent and be thought a fool than to open your mouth and remove all doubt.

Always try to drive so that your licence will expire before you do.

Oh Lord, let my words be sweet and tender, for tomorrow I may have to eat them.

To be right satisfies the ego; to be loving satisfies God.

I've recently re-read the book because, during Fr Ian's funeral, the Abbot quoted one of my choices:

When a Christian dies he goes from the land of the dying to the land of the living.

And reading the book has evoked so many memories. Witty comments, love poems, and challenging thoughts leap out from 10, 20, and over 30yrs ago. It's never too late to start collecting, so buy your book today!

I came across a quote from Mark Twain which could have been written for Fr Ian:

Let us endeavour to live so that when we die even the undertaker will be sorry.

How true is that for me? How true for you?

SPIRITUAL TOP-UP

As I was driving home yesterday, this little red light appeared on the dashboard - oil warning. Charles suggested (pretty strongly) that I should check it as soon as possible. So I did. Today. First thing. And I needed to add quite a lot of oil!! Because the bonnet of the car was up, I thought that I ought to check the water level too. A friend had stopped to talk to me, our cars drawn up alongside each other, and he had mentioned that he thought the car was over-heating. Sure enough, I needed to add water (and anti-freeze!)

I am the sort of person who gets in a car and drives. I tend to take it for granted, I do the petrol, but somehow I think that Charles will see that everything else is all right - until the lights flash. (I'm confessing this at great risk to peace and harmony in our home!)

Anyway, as I drove home, I began thinking about myself and my spiritual check-ups. Just as the car had warned me, so I could have personal warning lights too.

For example. I am very aware if I am losing the 'peace within'. If I am less tolerant and loving. The 'red light' comes on if I get into 'self justifying discussions' with the family. And sometimes it's family and friends who bring the warning, when they are willing to question my actions and motivation.

Before I drove to the garage, I got out the Owner's Manual for the car and checked up what *should* have been happening. Well written; easily understood; pictures and diagrams to help. It made correcting/solving the problems quite easy.

And for me? We're given a manual too. Well written; basic truths. Mine has lots of pictures and diagrams and footnotes for easy understanding. But I can't rely on someone else - it's up to me to maintain myself! So I'm off to do some checking up in my Bible to see how I *should* be.

I have a feeling that Charles will tell me that warning lights on dashboards never come on if the car is looked after properly - I guess that is true for people too.

The Spirit comes to set us free
and heal the broken hearted

A FREE GIFT

I switched on my car radio this morning to Premier Radio which is the Christian radio station for London, and I caught the end of an advertisement.

'Send now for your copy of The Holy Spirit and expect delivery within two weeks.'

Instinctively I felt there was some major theological error in this statement!! I started thinking about the Holy Spirit and how incredibly unique yet universal He is. We don't have to settle for 'copies' because we can have the original - exactly as He was (at the Beginning) and as He always will be (except you can't say 'until the end' as there won't be an End!)

And we don't have to 'send for Him' (with enclosed cheque or bank card) because He comes as a free gift; bringing many gifts for us so that we might help those around us. And His very presence produces fruit in our lives - love, joy, peace, patience, goodness, kindness, faithfulness, gentleness and self-control - that people might know that we are Christians.

Some of us don't really expect much of Him - He's always been around and we take Him for granted.

Some of us never opened the gifts He brought with Him, not realising that a gift is not a gift until both given and received.

And some of us are not allowing His fruit to grow; to let there be more of Him and less of ourselves.

And as for waiting two weeks for Him to come!! Isn't it wonderful that the moment we call out to Him, He is with us.

We have just celebrated Pentecost - the first time He came to those who waited (and they didn't even know what/who they were waiting for). He is likened to the wind and to flames of fire. And He was and He is and He will be.

And He is love and He is power - and He is in me and, I pray, that He is in you.

And I pray that others will see Him in us and ask to be introduced!

Zapped!   *Upper Room Feb.'94*

THE CHRISTIAN FAMILY

We've just returned from a family wedding and I was reminded that I was born into a family of which the members are very different, held together by bonds of love. There are two members left in my parents generation, eight in mine, twelve in the next (plus four husbands/fiancés) and Eliott the first of the latest!

It was fascinating to see how well the younger generation got on, and how some of their relationships had recently changed. We always get together at Christmas and various groups form - parents, school children, students, those earning their living - but this time, some had changed groups, and it was interesting to see the new relationships develop.

It made me think about relationships generally - how they do change. Usually because people or circumstances change or just because we mature or become more accepting of each other.

We're not a family that live close together or are in constant touch with each other, but when we are together it's as if we've never been apart. Isn't that how the Christian family should be? Not constantly together but bonded with a love so strong that even different styles, habits and visions are accepted. Each individual loved in their uniqueness - different talents appreciated and encouraged.

And then, surely, others will say - 'See how these Christians love one another' - and we will be fulfilling John 13:35. Isn't that what it's all about?

THE HEART OF BELIEF

On Sunday Charles and I worship at St Joseph's, the Catholic church, but on Wednesday I go to St Peter's, the Anglican church, so that I may receive Communion. The services are almost identical but every time I say the creed I think of the other church. There's a major difference, you see - in St Peter's we say 'I believe' whereas in St Joseph's we say 'We believe'.

I've been thinking about that a lot lately. I'm always pleased to say 'I believe' because then I'm telling God that I personally believe in Him and all that He has done for me. But when I say 'We believe', I feel closer to everyone around me and definitely part of His family, united in belief. I think that Protestants tend to over-emphasise their personal relationship with God and, maybe, Catholics are rather pre-occupied with their social commitments.

When I ask Jesus 'How much do you love me?' He stretches out His arms and says 'This much.' And the cross on which He is, has arms reaching out to the whole world.

Our relationship with our Father, the vertical, needs to be strong and immovable as that carries the horizontal - our loving concern for those around us.

Your place, and mine, is to be at the heart of the cross.

PROMISES

When I was little, I was a member of 'The Brownies' - I was an elf!
It was in the days of sack-like brown uniforms and leather belts
with purses attached; funny pull-on brown hats and bright yellow
bandannas which by intricate folding became beautiful ties. At the
beginning of every meeting there was 'an inspection' to make sure
we had put everything on properly; that we'd polished our shoes
and also our badges - the little gold ones that we received at our
enrolment and wore on our ties.

Our Brown Owl (the chief Brownie, for the uninitiated!) always
checked the shine on the back of our badges as well as the front.

She said that the badge should be like our promises - that they
should stand inspection from all directions. That's not a bad
guideline for life really.

The world, generally, says 'Promises are like pie-crusts, made to
be broken.' But Brown Owl's line - to stand inspection from all
directions - means not saying one thing and doing another. It
means, what's said today doesn't change tomorrow because I want
it to. It means being very careful before giving my word because
that word must be kept, even if it's hard and inconvenient. And it's
not just applicable to promises - it is also true for friendships;
commitments; lifestyles.

That statement really did affect my thinking and behaviour.
Later I discovered that the Bible says similar things:

The Lord detests lying lips but He delights in men who are
truthful. (Prov 12:22)

I try to be as true to my word as God is to his. (The Message)
2 Cor 1: 17)

and in Psalm 15:

Who may live on your holy hill?....... ....Who speaks the truth from
his heart and has no slander on his tongue......

Thank you Brown Owl for your words of wisdom all those years ago.

The Narrow Way

RUSHING TO JUDGEMENT

I am sitting in a garage waiting for my car to be fixed! Yesterday the engine kept cutting out whenever the car slowed down - e.g. at junctions; even just changing gear. Very dangerous indeed as that meant the steering wheel locked as well. Anyway, I have driven here in some trepidation because the traffic is pretty heavy and everyone seems to be in a hurry.

On the way I must have 'cut out' about 15 times and each time the drivers around me were very irritated. One lady stopped to allow me to join her traffic line and was then furious because I didn't move instantly. At one stage I had to get out and explain to the driver behind me what was happening as there was a danger of collision at the next roundabout if I couldn't move out smoothly.

I remember being in a traffic jam years ago and in my mirror I could see a red mini overtaking everything (on the wrong side of the road). I couldn't believe the stupidity of the driver, and had thought some most uncharitable thoughts, but as it drew alongside me I could see that it was a young man driving his very pregnant wife to hospital!! I resolved then to try not to judge a person's actions without trying to understand where they were coming from.

And I thought of that again today. The people around me had no idea of the difficulties I had. Even 'though I flashed the hazard lights in anticipation of the problem, they would still have no inkling of the cause. And why should they? They reacted out of ignorance and personal circumstances.

I must try to remember my earlier resolve to be understanding and tolerant of people's lives. I should try to remember that most people's unwanted actions come from some personal need or fault of nature which needs healing. Trouble is - we don't usually worry about our 'mechanical faults' but struggle on regardless.

The car will be fixed in an hour.
  - Oh that lives would be taken to 'The Mender' faster.
  - Oh that I would be slower to jump to the wrong conclusions!

In the beginning God created ....
Genesis 1:1

THE JOY OF BELONGING

We've just celebrated St David's day - the 1st of March. When I was young that meant a morning of pageant, poetry and music and then a half day holiday. It was one of the best days of the year, and we knew how fortunate we were to have been born Welsh.

Nowadays I just wear my daffodil with pride and take delight in smiling at complete strangers and wishing them a 'Happy St David's Day'. If ever I meet someone with Welsh connections, however small, we invariably try to find common ground, mutual friends or relatives. There's an intrinsic desire to 'be connected'. I realise that the Welsh are not perfect (well, not quite!), but we weather the teasing and jokes - and there are a lot of remarks this year about our rugby performances! - because, deep down there's a great feeling of worth and belonging to something wonderful.

One of the first scripture verses that Charles pointed out to me was Col 3:11 - 'Here there is no Greek or Jew, circumcised or uncircumcised, barbarian, Scythian, slave or free ......' to which he added ... 'Welsh or English!'

And I can accept that without any hesitation or problem. The reason why there is no division amongst the people is that however marvellous our natural race is, it is nothing compared with the joy, security and pride we feel at belonging to the family of God. And we do not have to look far for common ground when we meet each other, God is our Father, Jesus is our Saviour and His Holy Spirit lives within us.

What a joy of belonging. What a security of love we should experience. What a unity that should produce between us!

A BRIDGE TO GOD

Have you heard the latest teenage joke? Our sons persuaded us to use it when we were hosting a session at the CELEBRATE conference this year. It goes like this -

Charles said, 'Ask me if I am a bridge.'
I said, 'Are you a bridge?'
Charles looked puzzled. 'No' he replied.

Did you laugh? Probably not if you are over 20yrs old but for anyone younger, it really is the funniest thing they've heard this year. (No-one laughed at the Conference - admittedly the young people were at their own session - and Luke says we must have told it badly, but I don't see more than one way of telling it.)

Anyway, the funny thing is - I think we *are* bridges! As Christians we should be constantly helping people to reach each other in reconciliation or in overcoming prejudices. By the grace of God we should be able to bring people together, to facilitate forgiveness and by loving service (sometimes just by listening) we should be able to connect people, not only to people, but also to God.

Jesus gave his life that He might bridge the gap between us and our heavenly Father. That is the example of self-sacrifice which should be ever before us and only by the presence of His Spirit within can we hope to be used by Him.

The trouble is - bridges are made to be walked over, so get ready to be trodden on!!

SMALL THINGS

Our Christian Viewpoint committee was losing one of it's treasured members as Liza was moving to another area. The day before our last meeting I saw and bought a small box for her - on the lid it said 'SMALL THINGS' (it was only 4"x 4"x 2"). I 'phoned the other members and asked them to bring something small to put in the box. (This was after the shops had shut so it was up to them to find it at home!) And they were so clever and original:

A small card saying *'A good friend is one who knows where you've been, accepts you for what you are and encourages you to grow'.* And a reminder that *'God's sovereignty takes human obedience and accomplishes His will'.*

A box of matches with the note - *'A light to my eyes and a lamp to my feet.'* As God said *'Let there be light.'* Not Genesis again!' (Liza always returned to Genesis during every Bible study.)

A carved wooden mushroom representing our small group which will grow - and the fruit that is spread on the wind, the Spirit of God.

A lapel badge - a heart saying *'I love Israel'* - and a photo of Jerusalem as Liza so loves the Lord's chosen people and plans to return to Israel later this year.

A little mirror because Liza is a reflection of the glory of God.

A china dish with a beautiful butterfly to symbolise *'the transformed life we find in Christ and her new life just starting.'*

And a small piece of polished jade - *'make me like a precious stone giving glory back to you.'*

Everybody had been really challenged to find a gift from their own resources, and Liza was overwhelmed when she received the collection. Each thing special, small - possibly insignificant when taken out of context - but chosen in love and therefore meaningful and affirming.

Don't wait until someone is leaving - give a token of your love and esteem today.

Go on, face the challenge!

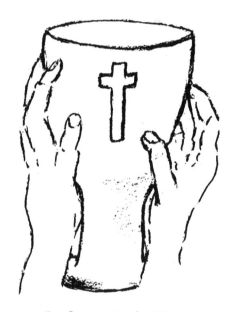

Cup Bearer to the King

UNCLOUDED JUDGEMENT

Luke is now ensconced in Leeds University to read Philosophy. I'm sure he'll have a wonderful time there and, hopefully, will find time for a little studying!

As we drove home after leaving him in the Hall, we were talking about the course he was taking and the people he would meet. For the first time in his life, everyone he'll be with will know him only as an adult. No-one will have childhood memories to affect their relationship - their friendship will be made or broken by who they are now. And this will be true for nearly all the students.

Sure, they're the product of the past and these next few years will shape them for the future, but they meet each other on equal footing without the encumbrance of past experiences.

Sometimes it's so very hard to stop memories colouring our relationships. I think that's why parents find it difficult to accept their children as adults - so often we remember all the immaturity, their youthful mistakes and bad judgements. And that is not just a parent - child thing. It permeates the spiritual realm as well when we sometimes find it hard to see a 'spiritual child' grow into a leader. (I know some people to whom Charles will never be more than an enthusiastic learner!)

It's very hard to move from a position of superiority (even if that's only by age) to one of equality. And so this is a time of challenge - to accept our grown-up children's opinions as those of adults. It doesn't mean agreeing necessarily, but it does mean respecting their view.

My problem is - the main topic on Luke's course this term is 'arguments'. He was pretty good before - heaven help me when he comes home for Christmas!

The Glory of God

CONCENTRATE YOUR MIND

I've just been to see the doctor. Nothing serious. I thought it could be, but it's not! Actually, I thought I was losing my mind, but apparently I'm not - not yet!!

The last straw happened when I couldn't find my trousers, which I'd hung behind the bathroom door. (Charles definitely hadn't touched them!) Eventually I tracked them down in my wardrobe but had no memory of how they got there. This seems to have happened a lot lately - a complete blank where memory should be.

Apparently this is normal! How many of you are now breathing deep sighs of relief?!! My doctor explained that my mind just didn't record what I'd been doing because I hadn't been concentrating.

So there you are. It's not the mind that's going, it's the concentration. Now that is a great consolation as I feel I can do something about it. I'm trying to focus on whatever I'm doing - and these last few days have been better. I've listened carefully when people talked to me and have been able to repeat the conversation to Charles, accurately. And I've worshiped and prayed in church without finding the service was over and I'd been thinking about Christmas cards or presents.

This is good news. And it just goes to show how a decision to concentrate makes a difference. So often we find ourselves in circumstances when it's easy to switch into 'automatic pilot'. Driving, praying - especially during a service. I challenge everyone to listen to what they are saying during the Creed and the Lord's Prayer. Today when I said, 'I believe in God the Father' I was overwhelmed by that statement and hours later I'm still thinking about the amazing fact that I believe!

Life has a new edge - a sharpness and beauty which I'd begun to take for granted. My mind might be older but it's not finished yet!

Alleluia!

THE CROSS

A friend of mine showed me the crucifix which is so precious to her. It was made of wood and silver and Christ's body was most delicately portrayed - silently suffering. And my reaction was - This is so beautiful. And it was. And yet afterwards I began to wonder - why was that my first thought? The cross has become so absorbed into our culture that it has even become the 'ultimate' fashion accessory. But in reality it is an object of horror, torture and obscenity.

I once attended a Good Friday service in our local church and the highlight, for me, was when four young men walked slowly down the aisle carrying a full-sized wooden cross. The wood was old, dirty and splintery. And the cross was heavy - the young men really felt it's weight. And when they dropped it into a hole in front of the altar, the thud echoed round the church. And I knelt, for the first time in my life, at the foot of the cross.

It was an overwhelming experience - even without the actual presence of Christ's suffering body, the magnitude and horror of his death came home. And yet, the crucifix can be beautiful. It is beautiful. Not because of an artist's impression; nor because it's aesthetically pleasing. No, it's only because we can glory in the cross of Christ. Because the cross is the symbol of what He did for us. It is His total unconditional love for us. And so Jesus transformed the most horrid and detestable thing into a symbol of hope and love. And I know that He wants to do that again and again in our lives.

I don't know how, I only know why - Because **HE LOVES.**

THE FAMILY OF GOD

A friend of mine took a young man with her to a J. John meeting. (J.John is a very well known Anglican evangelist in the U.K - an excellent speaker, very humorous and yet challenging.) His meetings are always very well attended and the atmosphere that night was animated and happy. The young man turned to my friend and said. 'Are all these people Christians? I thought you were a one off!'

Isn't it funny how one can live in an area for years and yet be totally unaware of the spiritual life that is happening all around? I remember how we lived here for nearly 5yrs; totally oblivious to the prayer groups, evening meetings and inter-church songs of praise going on around us. I was amazed to discover this 'spiritual strata' that existed when I met Jesus.

And I am aware that there are still people living here who have no idea that such things happen. That the vast majority of non-believers live their lives not overly curious about 'what goes on in the church.' What is the answer? Before we can invite people to 'come & see', we have to know them! We need to be meeting them where they are - joining them in their activities, their interests. And when we are friends - and when we have shown them how our lives are different because of Jesus - and when they have begun to wonder if there is more to life than what they have - THEN we can help them meet our lovely Lord and Saviour.

The young man I mentioned at the beginning is now a very committed Christian and knows that there are lots of us about.
I wonder who you will introduce to 'the family' this year?

UNCONDITIONAL LOVE

About 15yrs ago I saw a painting which I fell in love with. It was of the head and shoulders of Christ on the cross. The amazing thing is that the body was made up of heads of people, some famous and easily recognisable and others, like a baby, representative of a group. For many years I have thought of it and thought of how lovely to draw 'us' as 'the body of Christ'. Fr. Ian Petit used to tell us how at Mass, every time he said, 'This is my body ....' and then elevated the host at the consecration, he would look beyond and see the people - the body of Christ.

This year, Charles and I went to Australia and during a casual chat, I met someone who knew the picture. In fact, they knew someone who had it too! It originated in the U S A so I wasn't expecting that - I had never managed to find it at home. And my joy is now complete because I have a copy. But now that I have been able to sit and really look at it, I find it says something different - more than I realised before.

One of the recognisable faces is of Ghandi - and I know that he was not a Christian, so what does that mean? To me it means that Jesus took ALL of us onto the cross with him. Not just the Christians but even those who would never know him, would never acknowledge him. In fact, even those who would deny him completely. They were all there. He died for EVERYONE whether they know it or not. Even though he knew that his death would not make any difference to some people - he died for them anyway.

Now that is unconditional love.

SUNDAY CHRISTIAN

I recently heard a country and western song called 'Sunday Morning Christian' sung by Susan McCann. The chorus was the part that really made me think. Basically it told how Christians look and act 'so holy' on Sunday but, come Monday morning it's back to all the gossiping, cheating, manipulating ways of the world.

Quite a challenge! Is this really how non-christians see us? Is there any truth in the accusation? The song stated that we behave like this because we KNOW that God will always forgive us. And this knowledge is true. But we also know that we can't keep His forgiveness in a cupboard in anticipation of our need. That would be like holding our hand in the fire knowing that we have painkillers to take afterwards, and that would be ridiculous.

The danger is that, because we'll be forgiven, we don't worry about changing. The Sunday Morning Christian wore a 'Holy' mask on Sunday but the real self was what was seen the rest of the week. I must confess that I have talked to people who have implied the same thing - that Christians behave no better than others. In fact, often they are less loving and helpful than their 'pagan' neighbours.

Wouldn't it be wonderful if Christians were easily identifiable just by their behaviour? Did you know that in the early church the word 'Christian' was synonymous with 'kindness'? I wish that was always true today.

The answer must be that we should long to be different - to be changed. We must allow Him, who is always the same, to be seen in us. After all, we do believe He lives in us, don't we?

God WILL always forgive our lapses - but He would love us to be changed into the people he created us to be. Not Sunday morning Christians but the same yesterday, today and tomorrow.

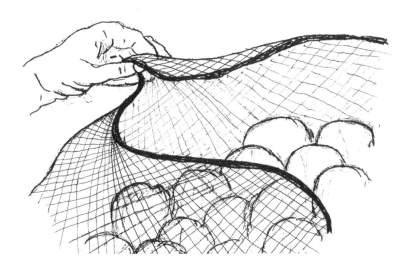

Alpha May '97

... I will make you fishers of men
Mark 1:17

SPEAKING POSITIVELY

We all know people who find it difficult to speak positively. You know, the ones who come up and say - 'You look terrible; are you O.K?'

I know that they are asking out of concern but if I'm not feeling 100%, I already know that I look awful and have probably spent longer than usual getting ready to try and do something about it!

Even worse is when someone says - 'I used to have a problem with you but I've been praying about it and God has really helped me to love you with His love.'

I really needed to know that!

Sometimes we need to examine our way of speaking to each other so that it is affirming and helpful. It's not always easy, but it usually improves with practice and conscious effort.

The old adage 'If you can't say anything nice, don't say anything' is helpful, but the difficulty comes when we are trying to say something nice and it comes out with negative undertones.

One of my worst offences is to say - 'You look much better today.'

'What do you mean 'today'? Didn't I look O.K yesterday? What was wrong? Did I look ill or are you talking about my clothes?' These thoughts are almost visible above my friend's head - and I was trying to be nice!

So maybe we just need to be careful not to say the first thing we think - this is very difficult for me! We need to concentrate on seeing only the positive and commenting on that, without the additions. If we see the problems, we must zip the mouth and realise that pointing out the obvious is not going to endear us to those we love.

I'm hoping that, with practice, I'll begin to think differently and only positive thoughts will be there. But until that time, all I can say is - 'God help each and every one of us!'

...the Spirit of God was hovering over the waters

Genesis 1:2

WASHED BY THE SPIRIT

Yesterday I cleaned the shower. Possibly other people clean theirs every week, even every day, but I'm a 'bath' person so I don't even notice the shower cabinet filming over. Even though the men in my life laboriously wipe it down after each shower (I hope that you're impressed by our teenagers' dedication!) a hard water film still manages to accumulate.

And it's pretty hard to shift. Using strong limescale cleaner and lots of elbow grease manages to achieve something, but the glass never returns to the pristine condition it was when we first installed it. It's because we live in a hard water area - a fact of life.

And Jesus said we lived in the world even if we were not 'of' it, so however hard we try, we are living in an environment which will 'dirty' us, just like the hard water 'dirties' the shower cabinet. Daily cleansing by prayers of repentance and forgiveness is going to show results but we also need deep cleansing by the Holy Spirit. And the longer we leave it, the harder the Spirit has to 'scrub'!

The Lord's been reminding me today of the 'film' that I've acquired. Most of it would be invisible to anyone else but I know it's there. I could ignore the Spirit's prompting and continue to appear OK, but really I would like to be as clean as possible so I'm asking Him to sort me out. It's a time of looking at ingrained habits and attitudes that are mine, not His - a time of challenge and surrender; a time of change. The joy is that He cleans far more effectively than we do - restoring us to true cleanliness.

Such is the power of His blood.

MOMENTOUS NIGHT

Charles and I greeted the new Millennium in church. We started with Mass at 8.00 p.m followed by a party in the church hall. Ages ranged from 5yrs to 'older' and everyone had a marvellous time with shared supper, lively music and old-fashioned games including Musical Chairs and Flip the Kipper.

At 11.00 p.m we returned to church for a short service, starting with a time of quiet reflection. And then, as we listened to Big Ben striking midnight, Fr Raphael lit the Jubilee candle. And from that single flame representing the light of Christ, we lit our candles and banished the darkness from the church. We sang, we exchanged greetings and peace and we prayed. And there was nowhere else that I wanted to be on that momentous night. In fact, as I knelt praying, I realised that I truly only wanted to be in church, in His presence.

And this is from the original IT girl! At University I was very busy either going to parties or organising them. People who knew me then would be surprised at the transformation in my life - I'm surprised myself! The difference is that then I lived life to the full - now I have the fullness of life.

So this is to encourage all parents who watch their children enjoying themselves with, apparently, very little time for the Lord. Keep up the prayers! Living life to the full without the Lord is not the answer, as we know - and, one day, they'll know it too!

STANDING MY GROUND

Today is St David's Day - patron saint of Wales! Many years ago, when I was leaving home (in Wales) to go to University (in England!) my father sat me down for a serious talk. He covered the need for me to study, to organise my money and to be true to all the values which he and my mother had taught me. And then he told me that I was never to be ashamed of being Welsh - even if I was teased or insulted. And if, on St David's Day, my tormentors said that I had to eat a raw leek - our national emblem - I was to do it without any fuss, in fact, I was to do it with pride! I'm not sure what had happened to him in the past but he obviously considered it necessary advice. In other words, I was never to be ashamed of my identity nor shrink from the consequences that that might bring.

Somehow those words gave me a format for my life, because when I became a Christian that is exactly how I felt about my identity in Christ. I am never ashamed of, nor try to hide, the fact that I am a child of God. I am a citizen of His kingdom and because of the Holy Spirit's presence within me, I have all I need to live out the ideals of our Heavenly Father.

It's quite interesting. I was rarely teased or taunted for being Welsh (I never had to eat the raw leek!) but I have been ridiculed for being a Christian and people have tried to push me to a limit to see my 'Christian' reaction. That's when I learn how serious I am about my faith - when the choice is popularity or truth I hope I'll go for truth every time!

A YEAR OF FAVOUR

Haven't the gardens been wonderful this year? I can hardly believe the amount of blossom on the trees - the lilacs and laburnums have been amazing. Even rhododendron bushes, that have been rather apologetic in the past, have been a riot of colour. There really have been 'hosts of golden daffodils' and carpets of bluebells to be enjoyed by all.

I know that it's because the weather has been very wet and mild, but I like to think that it's also because this is the year of Jubilee and God is showering us with His favour. Showing us, yet again, the beauty and profusion of His creation.

It really seems as if things are different this year, and not just in creation. Meetings, pilgrimages and conferences we have been to have been powerful. Our own conference, Celebrate 2000, was very blessed by the speakers, the music, the drama, the youth - in fact everyone who came contributed to the feeling of well-being, community and expectation. And I'm sure that the conferences yet to happen this year are also going to be 'different'. God is longing to meet us and act in our lives.

The translation '....the year of the Lord's favour' in Luke 4:19 is given as 'this is God's year to act!' in *The Message*. Let's help by having an expectancy of His presence with us - in our families, our church, our friends, our work. In our times together and also in our times of solitude and prayer.

I have no idea exactly what God has planned for us - but I bet it's challenging, exciting, beyond anything we could imagine and well worth doing. I think I'm ready - how about you?

MATERIAL SACRIFICES

Recently I revisited Durham - Charles and I met there while we were at the University but we left in 1965 so there were a few changes! The hills were definitely steeper and the distances between places seemed greater than when I was fit and young. But I had a marvellous time revisiting old haunts and remembering those halcyon days.

During my first year in Durham I lived opposite the Cathedral but I'm afraid I rarely visited it. I spent a glorious two hours there this time. It is a most beautiful building - majestic and yet not overpowering. But as I knelt in the choir stalls I was looking at lots of empty niches - not one statue to be seen - and I remembered why that was so.

Many hundreds of years ago the people of Durham were attacked and they sought refuge in the Cathedral. It was in the middle of winter and they were so desperate to keep warm that they began to burn the furniture in the church. Eventually there was nothing left to burn except their beautiful statues and so they were sacrificed too - a choice of life or death. And it did give them life because they were rescued. In memory of this, the statues were never replaced. A constant reminder of the need to sometimes sacrifice even that which is beautiful for God.

You can imagine where my thoughts went after that. What was there in my life that I should be sacrificing for the sake of my spiritual life? Were there 'idols' which needed to go? Was I willing to be stripped of my material belongings for the sake of 'life' or did I insist on the transient beauty of possessions? Quite hard questions - not yet fully answered - but an exercise not to be neglected if I'm serious about my future.

When I lived in Durham such thoughts never occurred to me - I didn't know Jesus then. I'm so grateful that now my life in Him is the only one that matters.

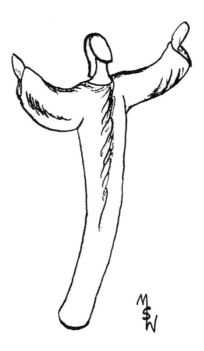

The father has sent the Son
to be the Saviour of the world
1 John 4:14   Easter '99

FACING CHALLENGES - WITH GOD

Recently I experienced one of the worst moments of my life, but I learnt something very important. I came downstairs and Paco, our cat, was staring fixedly at the small gap behind the corner cupboard in the hall. He had obviously lost the mouse he had brought in! Now, mice are not high on my list of favourite things, but, as I was on my own (except for Paco) it looked like I had a problem.

I closed all the doors off the hall and then moved the cupboard. The mouse ran out, past Paco, and under the door into the cloakroom. This is a very small room - about 6' x 3' - with a loo occupying half the ground space. I put Paco in there but he'd lost interest, so I was forced to go in myself!

For nearly 5 minutes I tried to persuade Paco to catch his 'friend' but he just wanted to play with him. The mouse ran everywhere - even over my feet! - and in the end I realised it was up to me to catch him. I'd taken a very small polythene box in with me and finally caught 'the monster' after several failed attempts. I cannot describe how I felt trying to catch a fast, wriggling, long tailed, furry creature in such a confined space.

What did I learn?

There are times when we have to face up to things we fear or dislike. There are times when, by an act of will, we have to over-come events or circumstances in which we find ourselves. I kept saying to myself - this is not life threatening, it's only highly unpleasant, but it will pass. Of course I prayed - desperate arrows of 'please let me do this quickly' - but God said 'You can do it. Just don't panic.'

Thank you, Lord, for the challenges of life - and the fruit of self-control!

I have been crucified with Christ....
Galatians 2:20   March '94

LOVE AND FORGIVENESS

Lucy was telling me about a very bad day she had with Eliott. There had been several occasions when she had been very cross with him and had ended up in the kitchen wondering what on earth she could do next! Eliott's head appeared round the door. 'In the book grandma gave me, it says that when you say you are sorry, everything can be alright again. And he disappeared!

I bought the book *You Are Very Special* by Su Box last year but had not realised it's such a firm favourite. Eliott has obviously understood the message that forgiveness is always available when we are sorry. He has made innumerable cards as a gesture of apology (prompted by pictures in the book!) and Lucy knows it's been a difficult day if he chooses it for his bedtime story!

Interestingly, I am reading a grown-up version about forgiveness - 'What's So Amazing About Grace?' by Philip Yancey. This book tells us, in different ways, about the love and forgiveness of God. How we can do nothing to make Him love us more, and how He promises never to love us less. If we can truly accept that grace is God's love for the undeserving, then our lives will proclaim it as powerfully as our words. I'm only half way through it, as it really is very challenging, but I am already more aware of my shortcomings in relating to those around me.

By the end I hope to be as confident in my relationship with God as Eliott is about his with his Mum! As his book says: 'Sometimes you do things that make people sad, but when you say sorry you can be friends again.' And as **HIS** book says: 'Forgive as the Lord forgave you. And over all these virtues put on love, which binds them all together in unity.' *(Col 3:13-14)*

AN ATTITUDE OF GRATITUDE

My father has just left on a rugby tour to Spain. He's 82yrs old so he's not playing, you understand, but is still an active and keen supporter. Last year he toured in Singapore, Kuala Lumpur and Penang and I'm hoping that this year's journey will be less eventful.

They were quite a large group, so the airline insisted on the team and supporters travelling separately - they were afraid of hooligans: rather an extreme expectation as so many of the group were in the 'very mature' age group! Anyway, Dad travelled from Cardiff to Amsterdam to connect with the flight to Asia. Unfortunately the plane was delayed because of bad weather and they missed the connection. Because it was 'an act of God' which caused the delay, the airline wouldn't accept responsibility, so my father and friends slept in the airport as best they could. Woken at 5.00 a.m by cleaners they were flown back to London to connect with a Malaysian Airline flight - finally reaching K.L nearly 24hrs late, to discover that their luggage had yet to join them!

Why I'm telling you this is because, as Dad was recounting it all to me, he just couldn't stop laughing. He has an amazingly positive attitude to life and manages to see the funny side of most problems - and that should be true for all Christians. Unfortunately it's not.

I was reminded of it this week when a dear friend told me that the Lord had told her that she should have 'an attitude of gratitude.' Isn't that a wonderful phrase? And if that becomes true for us - life will be a joy whatever our circumstances. Wherever we are, however we are, may we always look to our Heavenly Father with gratitude, joy and trust.

GOD AMONG US

I am feeling SO peaceful and amenable! This is because three weeks ago I helped organise a weekend retreat led by Fr Raniero Cantalamessa and, in spite of myself rushing around and being busy, I experienced the grace of God and a touch of His love.

Isn't it amazing that the Lord manages to do that? Of course it was made easier by Fr Raniero's brilliant teachings and by the atmosphere of worship and expectation during the sessions, but I still believe that He had been waiting for me to make myself available to Him and as soon as I did - there He was!

This morning I went to church for my communion service. During the service, just after the consecration, the church bell is rung for about a minute. This is as a signal to those outside that the Lord has come (at least, I think that's why we ring it!) The church is in the middle of the village so the bell will be heard by many people, but I wonder how many of them even notice? I sometimes wonder if the world, in general, has any idea of the presence of God amongst them? And yet, as I've learnt, He is SO close, SO eager, SO longing to touch us.

Because we know Him, we are looking for Him; but those around us, those 'not yet Christians', where will they find Him? Did you know that there are FIVE gospels and most people don't read the first four? They only read us! I really want to share this wonderful peace and tranquillity with everyone. It's got to be the answer for the unrest, disharmony and fighting going on around us. So my prayer is - May Your presence within me transform me into a person of such peace and love that others might long to know You too.

A PHONE LINE TO GOD

It was 8.15 am and the 'phone rang. Charles was away, speaking at a conference in Oxford, and when I answered I realised that someone was using a mobile 'phone - but no one spoke. For an awful moment I thought that maybe Charles had been involved in an accident and had only been able to press the 'home' button, but after calling him a few times and getting no response, I decided to listen and see if I could figure out what was going on. There seemed to be a group of people, including children, and cars - and then people getting into a car, slamming the doors and setting off.

A conversation started between two men (would you believe about the car they were in?!) and I finally recognised the voices as friends of ours, Peter and Myles. I realised that they were driving along the lane at Walsingham to the New Dawn Conference, which had started the previous day. And furthermore, Peter's 'phone had contacted me, unbeknown to him!

I started calling Peter's name and shouting 'Answer your 'phone!' but to no avail. The two of them continued their riveting chat - progressing into meaningful discussions about camping and getting stuck in rivers! I was fascinated but amazed that my strident tones were being ignored - I couldn't shout any louder; what else could I do to get his attention?

With that, Myles said that Peter could drop him off; so a few minutes later there was a quieter time with Peter driving on his own. I decided to whistle - a different approach and tone! I can't whistle - but I tried, badly, continuing to call his name as well. After two agonising minutes a little voice said 'Hello?'

'About time, too.' I said. 'It is now nearly 8.45 am and I have been trying to get you to answer the phone since 8.15.'

'What are you doing on my 'phone?' asked Peter in amazement.

I explained that, actually, he was on my 'phone and I related to him all that had happened. After we'd stopped laughing, a time which included some other exchanges - which are not relevant to this story - I said that I was very pleased to be talking to him as I'd been meaning to contact him about something anyway, but knowing that he was away for the week, I'd decided to wait until later.

When I was telling Charles about it later I realised what it showed me about my relationship with God, my Father. Sometimes I open a 'phone-line to Him - maybe by an arrow prayer, a shout for help, an action or reaction, I don't know, - but somehow He is waiting to continue the conversation with me and I am otherwise engaged. He goes to a lot of trouble to get my attention but my mind is so absorbed by the minutiae of my day that I just ignore His promptings. It's only when I find myself alone, with time to think about His plans that I become aware of the small quiet voice that hasn't given up calling my name.

The world is so hectic and distracting these days - let's take some time out and give God a chance.

JOY IN THE LORD

A well-known preacher was talking to his congregation about heaven and hell. It went something like this:

'When I speak of Heaven,' he said, 'try to let your faces show the happiness that you feel inside. But when I speak of Hell – your normal faces will do.'

I was thinking about that again when I was in church this week. I do find it strange that people, who have just received the Lord in communion, walk back to their seats looking worried, sad or generally unhappy! It is amazing what has just happened – that moment of grace when heaven and earth are united. Awesome! How can we be anything but overwhelmed with the knowledge of God's love and filled with joy at the realisation of our acceptance by him, through Jesus?

And, maybe, our faces could show it!

I must confess that sometimes I want to dance back to my seat (O.K, so I'm an Anglican!) but I can't help smiling at those around me. And several people look at me and respond with beams of joy – we know that this is a moment of supreme happiness and we are delighted to share it with someone.

On Sundays, when I go to receive a blessing, I always turn my face upwards (symbolically towards my Father in Heaven) and smile as I receive his love. Similarly, at the end of Mass, I 'look up' to that love about to descend on me as the priest blesses us and sends us out. Whenever I ask my earthly father for something – or know that he is about to give me something – I always look into his face, as I know that there I will see his love for me. Why should it be different when I am thinking of God?

Maybe it's time we let our bodies show our emotions more. Maybe it would be alright to show that we have joy and peace that is not of this world. Maybe people would respond to us differently - maybe they're just longing to share something but don't know how.

And maybe, just maybe, that moment of earth and heaven uniting will stretch into the whole day and our faces will show that thoughts of Heaven bring joy, excitement and happiness, always.

Wouldn't that be great?

'Our Daily Needs'

Then Jesus declared, 'I am the bread of life.
He who comes to me will never go hungry, and
he who believes in me will never be thirsty.'
John 6:35

TRADITION

A young wife decided to boil some ham for supper. Her new husband watched her prepare it, but was curious as to why she cut a corner off. She explained that her mother had done it, but she didn't know why. She telephoned her mother the next day and asked her to satisfy his curiosity. The mother thought for a moment and then replied that she wasn't sure, but her mother had always cut a piece off and she was just carrying on the tradition. The young wife was not satisfied with that so she went round to visit her grandmother and asked her the same question.

And do you know what the answer was?   The grandmother had never had a pan big enough to hold a piece of ham!!

I loved that story when I heard it about four years ago – during a homily! And I remembered it this week because I wondered if we sometimes do things without thinking or understanding why.

So often we just follow what everyone else does so that we 'fit in'. But if we know why we do things, it doesn't matter whether other people do them, or not!

Basically I find myself alone, during Mass, making the sign of the cross at the end of the Creed. This is because when I was being prepared for confirmation, I was taught to cross myself then. As I have just stated what I believe, I should also say to God – 'I commend to you my thoughts, my body, my strength and my heart.' I always finish by placing my hand on my heart!

Do we really understand why we do things – if we do they enrich our lives. If we don't, they're meaningless.

LISTENING TO THE SPIRIT

Written above my desk is the following prayer:

God, help me to try
not to RUN everything,
But if You need help, just ask!

I think that would be known as a contradiction of intent!

Of course I mean it when I acknowledge that my desire to organise everyone around me – often to their annoyance – is a fault. On the other hand, I feel that God has given me certain administration gifts and I want to use them for Him. Is this a problem? Not for Him, only for me!

I am grateful that grace builds on nature, but sometimes our nature needs purifying first. If I try to take over because I feel it's only my way which is right – that's obviously wrong. But if I'm prompted to suggest an alternative, and then be relaxed if it's refused, I think that's OK. It really is quite hard to know what my motive is – and I'm glad you won't read this until after Celebrate when my 'suggestions' will have been multiple!! I needed Anne to turn to me during registration last year and say 'I really can do this on my own, you know,' to recognise my interfering quality! (and she was so right.) We often don't even know when we're being a problem – that's why God has given us friends and families who love us enough to tell us!!

I don't think I'm alone in this quandary of mixed motives although other people might have different examples of 'nature changing' needed.

I have enough of a problem dealing with my own than to worry about yours, but it certainly is a salutary exercise to consider how God sees our actions - are they truly done out of love for Him and those around us or are they done out of our own capabilities and pride?

An interesting question to leave with you, as I turn my attention to Charles's office. Would I dare? !!

.... And all the people listened attentively
to the Book of the Law
Nehemiah 8:3

WAIT FOR THE LORD

Charles and I are leaving for Australia tomorrow, and I must write this column before I go! It's a funny thing about *The Other Half* – I really do have to wait for inspiration to strike, and I'm often on my knees reminding God that 'this is the deadline day' and Kristina will be ringing me to find out where it is!

Anyway, recently I was talking to someone who was trying to sell their house. They were very concerned because they had had very few people looking at it, but I pointed out that you only need one person to buy the house, so who needs the inconvenience of lots of others viewing? Try to relax! I think that's how God works sometimes – there's no sign of anything happening and then, suddenly, it all comes together.

I think it works like this – God always answers our prayers straight away, but sometimes he gives the answer to Fred – a tortoise. Fred sets out with the answer, very slowly, and as long as we keep praying and expecting the answer, Fred keeps moving. But when we stop, Fred stops! That's why nothing appears to be happening. But God really has it all under control and the answer will arrive at the right time.

So, if we are trying to live our lives in God's plan, we can trust him to keep us on the right path. We mightn't see a lot of activity, but then, after all, we only need the final solution.

It's not always easy to wait patiently for the Lord to act, but at least we know that He loves us and wants to be involved in our lives. How hard it must be to live without the knowledge of His love when times are hard. The hope we have while waiting far outweighs the despondency of helplessness we would otherwise experience.

Thank you, Lord, for lovingly meeting my needs - especially *The Other Half*, today!

It's beginning to rain

GOD HAS NO FAVOURITES

A friend of ours recently attended a Catholic conference in beautiful surroundings and with excellent teachings. When Charles asked him what had been the highlight for him, he said that it was the blessing that he had received during the distribution of the Eucharist. He attends Mass regularly with his family, although he is not a Catholic, so he could be said to be a connoisseur of blessings – and this was one of the best he'd ever received. I must confess that the quality of blessings one receives does vary considerably!

The priest who blessed him had a truly ecumenical heart, and that makes a difference. My friend said that you can tell a lot about a person by the blessings they give and this priest totally accepted him as a brother.

To be truly ecumenical is quite rare, I think. Most of us say we are, but underneath the surface we do not really accept people where they are with God. We have a sneaking feeling (hope) that, one day, they will see the light! Much of this arises because we do not know nor understand what they believe. Sometimes we feel they don't understand and accept us, so why should we bother? We need to bother, because God wants His children to love each other.

It's important to remember that God loves all His children – He has no favourites. If we want to work with our brothers and sisters we need to accept them just where they are – we don't need to agree about everything, what family does? But we do need to trust them and get to know them better. It is often easier to stay within our own groups instead of venturing out to try and break down barriers – especially if life is pretty hectic anyway!

I believe, the Lord wants to bless all the things in which we are involved for Him. But if we have worked with other Christians across the great divide and encouraged each person in total acceptance – Charles and I have found the blessing increases immensely.

Being part of a large family is wonderful – it would be a pity not to know our relatives!

(Thinking of our natural families might not be a helpful analogy – you might not want to see some of your relatives all the time! – but when it comes to brothers and sisters in the Lord, I think He'd like us to meet them as often as possible.)

SMILE - GOD LOVES YOU !

I've just been speaking to a friend of mine and, in the course of conversation, she suddenly said 'I saw something really funny the other day. I was driving along and I saw a sign at the side of the road which said

HOMEMADE SAUSAGES
100 YARDS LEFT'

The two of us burst out laughing! – much to the amusement of the shoppers around us. I'm sure that not everyone will find that amusing – O.K, we might have a strange sense of humour – and I'm sure hundreds of people will have driven past the sign without a second thought or chuckle.

Humour is a funny thing (no pun intended!). I must confess that modern alternative comedy leaves me cold. I think it's because most of it involves laughing AT someone or making someone uncomfortable. I really dislike negative humour which is always at someone else's expense, but that seems to predominate in entertainment these days.

Maybe we could start a campaign and only laugh at jokes which don't embarrass anyone, don't put someone down nor cause offence. The trouble is, I suspect we won't be laughing very much, so here are a few gentle giggles to start you off.

A man goes into the cinema and buys a ticket for himself and his dog. The usher is amazed to see the dog laughing throughout the film. After the show she says to the man 'I was surprised to see your dog laughing at the film.' 'So was I,' replied the man, 'he hated the book.'

A monastery in the English countryside had fallen on hard times and decided to establish a business to defray their expenses, such as a bakery or winery. However, being English they decided to open a fish-and chips restaurant. The establishment soon became very popular, attracting people from all over. One city fellow, thinking himself clever, asked one of the brothers standing nearby, 'I suppose you're the fish friar?' 'No,' answered the brother levelly, 'I'm the chip monk.'

An atheist was lying in the funeral parlour. The mortician put the finishing touches to the body and sighed, 'Look at him – all dressed up and nowhere to go.'

Sorry if you've heard them before – but a good joke always bears repeating! Feel free to share.

The Admiral on the bridge of a large naval ship saw a light ahead, set for collision with his vessel. He signalled to it: 'Alter your course ten degrees south.' Back came the reply, 'Alter your course ten degrees north.' The Admiral tried again. 'Alter your course ten degrees south, I am a captain.' The reply was 'Alter your course ten degrees north, I am a Seaman third-class.' The Admiral, furious by now, signalled back: 'Alter your course by ten degrees south. I am a battleship!' The reply? 'Alter your course ten degrees north. I am a lighthouse.'

A farmer went to market to buy a new horse and the one he chose was a beautiful animal. 'There are only two words you need to remember for this animal,' said the seller. 'He was previously owned by a charismatic, so he stops when you say 'Amen' and will start galloping when you say 'Alleluia'.' The farmer decided to ride him home and all was going well until he decided to go for a gallop along the cliff top. The horse went faster and faster until it's rider became a little frightened but in his panic he could not remember the 'stop' word. He tried everything and eventually he shouted 'Amen' and the horse stopped immediately, right on the edge of the cliff. The farmer shook with relief. 'Alleluia,' he said...........................

Set my heart on fire

MADE WITH LOVE

Do you know that no one sells pram-sets for doll's prams anymore? You know, pillows, sheets and covers. In this hi-tech age, no one sells them. I'm sure children still play with them – in fact, I know they do as there has been a request for them this Christmas, and I have spent the last two days making them!

I thought it would be an easy, straightforward job. I bought the material, cut it up, tacked it together, got out the machine – and that's when it all went wrong. The machine had not been used for a LONG time so it made weird noises and I had to take it apart and oil it before continuing. Then the tension was wrong which meant a lot of adjusting – I managed to lose the balance completely and caused even more problems.

But now I've finished, it's all worthwhile. In the 'old days' I wouldn't have wasted my time going to the shops to try and buy the set. I would have just got on and made it. These days we are so used to having everything prepared for us – our clothes, our food, our entertainment. Everything has to be quick, slick and perfect.

Well, Amelia is going to have a unique set for her pram this year. It's not mass-produced - no brand name! It's certainly not perfect, but it's been made with lots of love. Now, what else can I try?

Maybe I can look at my spiritual life. Do I always look for the ready-made, the mass produced schemes, some-one else's vision? Or shall I go back to basics and find my own way? I might need to 'oil a few thought processes', to reset my priorities to regain the perfect balance, but I'm sure that afterwards I'll find that the best, for me, will be unique and personal and full of His love.

WHO ARE YOU?

We usually find it helps to put people into pigeonholes, don't we? When we first meet someone, it does help if we can put them into a neat box of relationship, work or habitat – it helps us to remember them, and something about them for future reference. But sometimes it goes too far.

We used to have a dog; a Tibetan Terrier called Yorrick. (Yes, I know, 'alas, poor Yorrick' – always a sad moment when we took him to see the vet!) He was actually quite a good example of the breed, so the breeder persuaded me to show him a few times. One of these was at the Lady's Kennel Club, which was held at Earl's Court. Charles had dropped us off and returned later to collect us. He came into the hall and was immediately surrounded by the amazing noise of hundreds of dogs - and their owners! He finally found a lady holding a Tibetan Terrier and enquired where the breed was showing.

'Who are you?' She asked.
'Charles Whitehead' he replied.
'No, no' she said. 'What's your dog's name?'
'Oh, that's Yorrick' said Charles.
'Oh, - you're Yorrick's Daddy' she beamed – and took him to where we were.

That little episode encouraged me to stop pigeonholing people. I really felt it was going a bit far!

I've been put in lots of pigeonholes during my life – Terry's daughter; Jane's sister; Lucy's Mum. Even 'the other half'! I've never minded any of them. In fact they've identified me in roles

I've loved – but, sometimes, they've helped me hide from who I could be. Having an easily identifiable role gives me such comfortable parameters of life that I don't always find it easy to look for God's direction for myself. Sometimes He asks me to step out of my present position – that's scary. Occasionally He wants me to take new decisions – that's difficult; and I've even heard Him whisper 'If you're the other half of Charles, which bit am I?' – that's very sobering.

So, I am the other half - but not really half! More like one of two pieces that fit together very well – with a BIG heart-shaped space in between for the Lord: knowing that each of our identities is unique and important to Him, and that He has plans for us both – separately and together.

And I wonder - have I been pigeonholing God? Now THAT'S a worrying thought!

Treasure in jars of clay

EPILOGUE

I hope you don't mind if I add another bit to the previous chapters. This book has really grown over quite a long time. As I re-read the early bits I realise that the children have grown up now and a lot of the stories happened a long time ago. For example - please don't ask Luke, if you meet him, if he still loves Hobnobs, I think his taste has changed a bit! But one thing hasn't changed at all - the faithfulness of God and His ability to surprise me every day. He is amazing!

Looking back over my own life I can see that He has been close to me all the time. Even when I went to Durham University and decided, in the infallible wisdom that all teenagers possess (you must know the saying - if you have a problem, ask a teenager because they know everything!) that God didn't really exist, His hand still protected me and guided me. That's where I met Charles and we were married a year after leaving.

Suffice to say that twelve years later when God showed me He DID exist - I got so excited that I've been trying to tell people about Him ever since. But the most important thing I've learnt is that my relationship with Him is different to what I thought it should be many years ago. When I was growing up - going to Sunday school, being confirmed - I thought I had to try to imitate Jesus; I had to grit my teeth and love everybody. And I knew that was impossible! But God showed me that it isn't like that, not at all.

You probably know that verse in the Bible about jars of clay: For God, who said, 'Let light shine out of darkness,' made his light shine in our hearts to give us the light of the knowledge of the glory of

God in the face of Christ. But we have this treasure in jars of clay to show that this all surpassing power is from God and not from us.' *(2 Cor 4: 6-7)*

When I heard that, I couldn't see how treasure in a jar was going to be seen by anyone - but God said that I was thinking of the wrong kind of jar. Think of a jar with holes in - you know, the ones you put nightlights in. You see, all men are created by God, whether they know it or not, but in Christians there is a treasure - the light of Christ has been lit. We are just the jars of clay, but we were created to hold that light and so until the light is lit, we are not complete, we are not fulfilled. But when we are carrying that treasure, our responsibility is to let His light be seen. We need to keep those holes clear - and they get blocked quite easily. Blocked by things we do, things done to us and, of course, by sin. Time and time again we need to come in humility, in forgiveness, in repentance - and again and again the light will shine even more brightly and Christ will be seen in us. It's amazing - His love will be noticeable in us! We really will love people, not pretending but really - because He said He would live in us and so He does, and if we let it, His love will flow.

I'll tell you something else I learnt. I have a small jar of clay (with holes in!) and I often light a small light in it and sit with it in the dark thinking about the wonders of our God. I broke it. Not a huge break, but a small triangle broke at the top, and do you know what? - more of the light could be seen! How about that? We so often think that our lives have to be perfect to witness as Christians. We try to cover up the problems we have, to pretend that everything's fine. But God said that if we give Him the brokenness, if we surrender our problems to Him, He can use them. Sometimes He mends the broken bits, but sometimes, if we let Him use them, more of His light will be seen in us. Isn't that fantastic? I think about it nearly every day. I am a clay jar and

I mustn't detract from Christ's presence within me. When people look at me, do they see me or Jesus? Being a Christian makes me different because I carry a treasure, not for myself but for those I meet, I really can bring light to others - the light of the world.

I hope this book has done a bit of that. I've shared some of the weird and wonderful things that have happened to me, my family and friends, in the hope that you'll see that God is very close to everyone. He is everywhere, in everything and longs for each of us to want to know Him better – and the more we know, the more we realise we don't know. But that's all right – He has all eternity to share with us and that's plenty of time!

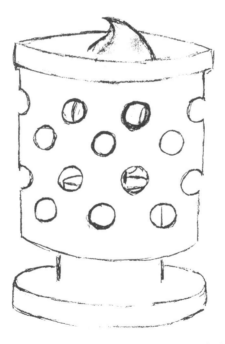

But we have this treasure in jars of clay...
2 Corinthians 4: 6-7

Further copies of this book
may be purchased from

Goodnews Books & Audio
15 Barking Close
Luton, LU4 9HG
England

Tel: 01582 571011
Fax: 01582 571012

email: orders@goodnewsbooks.net
www.goodnewsbooks.net

Goodnews is a mail order and
internet Christian book service